Awareness Is the Start of Breakthrough

LIFE'S GREATEST BATTLES

REBECCA BRAND

LIFE'S GREATEST BATTLES
Copyright © 2019 by Rebecca Brand

ISBN 978-1-9997955-8-0
Printed and bound in the United Kingdom.

All rights reserved.
No part of this publication may be reproduced, stored in a retrieval system, or transmitted in any form or by any means, electronic, mechanical, photocopying or otherwise, without prior written consent of the publisher except as provided by under United Kingdom copyright law. Short extracts may be used for review purposes with credits given.

Main translation in use:
Unless otherwise indicated, all Scripture quotations are taken from the Holy Bible, New Living Translation, copyright © 1996, 2004, 2015 by Tyndale House Foundation. Used by permission of Tyndale House Publishers, Inc., Carol Stream, Illinois 60188. All rights reserved.

Other translations in use:
Scripture quotations marked NKJV are taken from the New King James Version®. Copyright © 1982 by Thomas Nelson. Used by permission. All rights reserved.

Scripture quotations marked NIV are taken from THE HOLY BIBLE, NEW INTERNATIONAL VERSION®, NIV® Copyright © 1973, 1978, 1984, 2011 by Biblica, Inc.® Used by permission. All rights reserved worldwide.

Scripture quotations marked ESV are taken from The ESV® Bible (The Holy Bible, English Standard Version®). ESV® Text Edition: 2016. Copyright © 2001 by Crossway, a publishing ministry of Good News Publishers. The ESV® text has been reproduced in cooperation with and by permission of Good News Publishers. Unauthorized reproduction of this publication is prohibited. All rights reserved.

Scripture quotations marked TPT are from The Passion Translation®. Copyright © 2017, 2018 by Passion & Fire Ministries, Inc. Used by permission. All rights reserved. ThePassionTranslation.com.

Scripture quotations marked HCSB are taken from the Holman Christian Standard Bible®, Copyright © 1999, 2000, 2002, 2003, 2009 by Holman Bible Publishers. Used by permission. Holman Christian Standard Bible®, Holman CSB®, and HCSB® are federally registered trademarks of Holman Bible Publishers.

Scripture quotations marked MSG are taken from The Message, copyright © 1993, 2002, 2018 by Eugene H. Peterson. Used by permission of NavPress. All rights reserved. Represented by Tyndale House Publishers, Inc.
Emphasis within Scripture quotations is the author's own.

Published by
Maurice Wylie Media
143 Northumberland Street
BELFAST
Northern Ireland
BT13 2JF (UK)

Publishers' statement: Throughout this book the love for our God is such that whenever we refer to Him we honour with Capitals. On the other hand, when referring to the devil, we refuse to acknowledge him with any honour to the point of violating grammatical rule and withholding capitalisation.

For more information visit
www.MauriceWylieMedia.com

DEDICATION

To my daughter Sarai,
my prayer is that you will never know the battles life can throw at you because you will walk in true freedom for all of your days.

CONTENTS

Introduction 7

Chapter One : What Is Our Purpose? 11

Chapter Two : How Do We Become Disciples? 21

Chapter Three : Does God Actually Exist? 43

Chapter Four : Suffering with a Loving God 69

Chapter Five : It's Them, Not Me! 93

Chapter Six : Broken but Healed 111

Chapter Seven : Do You See Me? 132

Chapter Eight : The Atomic Bomb 150

Chapter Nine : Jesus' Number One Topic 173

Chapter Ten : Yes, We Should Love Sex 198

Chapter Eleven : Rise and Shine 219

Chapter Twelve : It Looks Good on You 232

Notes 250

Acknowledgments 259

About the Author 261

INTRODUCTION

'So if the Son sets you free, you will be free indeed'. John 8:36 NIV

From the point of accepting Christ into our hearts we have a choice to live in the freedom that Christ died for. We also then have an option to obtain the fullness of God's love and to journey with Him to fulfil our God-given purpose—so what is it that stops us from receiving that freedom?

In a world that seems to tear people down or want to strive for the impossible, we have become a race that is looking for that 'quick fix' rather than journeying through life together. This can result in us not recognising the person staring back at ourselves in the mirror, let alone who God created us to be.

This book brings awareness to the issues that most of us are facing, and yet we don't know where to turn. Ashamed, feeling broken, alone, and most of the time feeling out of control, the truths revealed here will bring light to the darkness and freedom from those invisible chains.

One day I asked God a straightforward question as to why there are so many people who are unsure how to break free from the pain or strongholds within their lives. I was shocked by the answer.

Life's Greatest Battles was written from my heart to see people set free from the strains of life. My passion is to encourage people to realise that God created us for "such a time as this"; and until the body of Christ fulfils what God created us to do, Jesus won't return.

The same topics always keep coming up within my world, and I realised that I had received breakthroughs from these issues that so many people are struggling with, such as rejection, comparison, shame, uncertainty, suffering, offence, and generally feeling broken by life. I now believe that I can show others how to break free from these strongholds too.

Within this book, I also tackle the battles we face with money, sex, and how to win the conflicts. Because many of us may be facing them alone, because we are too afraid to speak out, in fear of being judged or not being understood.

Every chapter of this book comes from my personal experience; but more importantly, the Word of God. I wrote this book to show people that freedom is available to each one of us. Even in my darkest hours, God still found me, and He will do the same for you too.

I have discovered that half of the battle is realising there is a battle in the first place! After all, satan came to steal, kill, and destroy. Unfortunately even we Christians have fallen for his lies.

Introduction

God wants us all to live in abundance, walk in freedom, and to love people wholeheartedly within this world. If we aren't doing that, then I believe true liberty doesn't yet exist in our lives. To date, there are 2.3 billion Christians in a world of 7.3 billion people. To me that says it all, because Jesus says to "Follow Me"; therefore, when we do find the freedom that Christ provides, we should want everyone else to receive it as well.

For years, I have felt like there is pretence of needing future generations to see the revival through, but also, that those alive today, were to pass on the baton. Yet I strongly believe that Christians are required to rise up now, because Jesus is coming, and it is never too late to step into your God-given calling!

My heart breaks when I read about the parable of the Ten Virgins in Matthew 25:1-13 because it shows that not everyone will be ready for the return of Jesus; and yet, God created everyone with the choice to be with Him for all of eternity. My passion is, therefore, to see more people have that eagerness, and to be ready for Christ.

My prayer is that you will read this book and start the journey of becoming aware of the battles the enemy has tried to hide from you. And to discover what true spiritual breakthrough looks like in life. This book shows how we can honestly walk in freedom when biblical viewpoints and Scripture are applied to our everyday lives.

I have struggled along these different paths for years; but now, after writing this book, I walk in real freedom. God brought me through this journey, and I want to encourage you to do the same.

This book started as a voyage to be obedient to God, but instead has been life changing for me personally, because knowing that we have freedom from Christ and actually walking in that true freedom is the difference between living in our destiny and merely existing until we die. I now know my purpose and destiny. Will you go through the same journey to discover yours?

Let's shine in the darkness and be all that we were created to be, with purpose and clear direction.

Let's change the world with hope.

Let's do this together.

Rebecca

CHAPTER ONE

WHAT IS OUR PURPOSE?

Discovering Why God Created Us for this World

> *'When you realise God's purpose for*
> *your life isn't just about you,*
> *He will use you in a mighty way'.*
> *Dr Tony Evans*

Why Were We Created?

How many of us know what our God-given purpose is? Like, why God decided to create a human called _____ (insert your name) that has your unique character, looks, and even quirks. God thought the world needed someone like you!

Think about it. God wrote all of your days in His book (Psalm 139:16) and He knew that today you would start to read, *Life's Greatest Battles*. How remarkable is that?

Being honest, I did not understand what my purpose was in God's ultimate cosmic plan until 2014. Not because He didn't want me to find out, but more, it never crossed my mind that *our lives* weren't about *us*.

God created us, specifically for this time, and everyone we meet or have a relationship with will help shape us in some way. It blows my mind that this day has now been 'ticked off', and this part of the plan has now been achieved. The Bible says that *anything* that happens in this world, God knew about before the beginning of time:

> '...*I am God, and there is none like me. Only I can tell you the future before it even happens. Everything I plan will come to pass...*'. Isaiah 46:9-10

The Bigger Picture

I wrote this chapter to get us thinking, because only you and I can accomplish the purpose that God created specifically for us; therefore each believer is just as important as Jesus returning. If we are still breathing, then God's plan for us is still unfolding.

Therefore, I want to unpack what our purpose is and to realise that *life isn't about us*. It is more about our relationship with God and speaking to Him through prayer. I will also go through my thoughts as to why I feel this is important later in the chapter.

Lastly, I want to explain the different ways that we can speak to other people about Jesus, because that was, after all, the mandate that Jesus left for us to do!

As individuals, God wants us to be intimate with Him; but collectively, together, we play an essential role in eternity.

In the Beginning

Have you ever wondered what life (or even the world) would have been like if Adam and Eve had not eaten the fruit from the Tree of Knowledge in the Garden of Eden? (Genesis 3)

Adam and Eve experienced what it was like to be able to live in God's presence daily, and to be in a place of continual abundance and love. To this day, that plan for humanity has never changed. He still desires for *all of His children* to be with Him, walking with Him every day. That includes every person who has ever lived, is currently alive, and is yet to be born. God's desire was and is that every one of us would be with Him.

But sin separated Adam and Eve and us from God until Jesus died on the cross. Meaning that there was then a way to come back into an intimate relationship with God and fulfil what we had been created to do in the first place.

Finding God's Grace

For years I used to think that 'sin', sounded like a nasty or even harsh word. It made me feel 'dirty' and not good enough to be a Christian.

Back in 2006, I had just found God; and at that time, I had been an atheist for 25 years. I was at a place in my life where I had discovered there was, in fact, a heavenly Father, who had created everything I knew around me.

I loved God so much, but because I felt like I was doing things wrong, I just assumed I was going to hell anyway because I remember thinking that I was never going to meet up to 'God's standards', so what was the point in trying?

I realise now that my viewpoint of God was incorrect. I had not accepted that Jesus dying meant that God's grace was unmerited. I did not deserve it, but I couldn't earn it either because God gives it to us freely and without conditions.

Someone later told me that the meaning of sin was 'outside of God's will', because He is holy and righteous, and therefore He cannot stand to be in the presence of sin. That is why God had to send Jesus to die at Calvary; He needed to make a way when there was none. The Old Testament law was merely for humanity to realise that the Israelites needed a Saviour.

Humanity as a whole needed someone else to take our sins away because we would always continue to sin due to our inherited nature from Adam. No matter how hard we tried, we would never be sinless.

Jesus' atonement means He takes our sins away from our past, present, and future. Jesus makes us pure in God's eyes so that we can enter into a loving, intimate relationship with Him.

Unfortunately, there are so many of God's children in the world who are yet to meet God personally. As mentioned previously, in 2015, there were 2.3 billion Christians in a world of 7.3 billion people.[1] Most of these people have heard about Yahweh, *'the name above all other names'* (Philippians 2:9). Despite this, Christianity sees limited growth in certain countries and within Europe, there has even been a decline. Why? In my opinion, perhaps people are not sharing the gospel in the way that Jesus asked of us.

In the Gospels, Jesus said:

What Is Our Purpose?

'Therefore, go and make disciples of all the nations, baptising them in the name of the Father and the Son and the Holy Spirit. Teach these new disciples to obey all the commands I have given you...'. Matthew 28:19-20

Jesus commissioned His eleven disciples (Matthew 28:14) to go out into the nations and make disciples.

What Is a Christian?

Did you know the word "Christian" is found only three times in the New Testament?

1. Acts 11:26; *'And when he had found him, he brought him to Antioch. So it was that for a whole year they assembled with the church and taught a great many people. And the disciples were **first called Christians** in Antioch'.*
2. Acts 26:28 (NKJV); *'Then Agrippa said to Paul, "You almost persuade me to become a **Christian**".'*
3. 1 Peter 4:16 (NKJV); *'Yet if anyone suffers as a **Christian**, let him not be ashamed, but let him glorify God in this matter'.*

In reading these Scriptures, did you notice that it was not Jesus who was using the word 'Christian'? Have you ever wondered why? The reason being, it was derogative terminology used by the Romans to belittle and demean the people who were following Jesus.

The word Jesus used was 'disciple', and disciple means 'to follow, to do what He does'! And to be anyone's disciple comes at a cost. I hear you thinking the gift of eternal life is free to anyone who asks

Jesus to come into their lives (John 3:16). Yes, that is true. But it does require us to recognise that 'counting the cost' (Luke 14:25-34) means agreeing to what is actually taught by Jesus and not just picking out the good bits; Christianity is not a buffet where we can pick and choose the things that seem appealing to us.

Jesus never demands anything of us in order to control His followers. This would go against the very reason that God created humanity with free will in the first place, which is the right to choose and act at our discretion. But more, if we love Jesus, the natural path is to want to please Him by following His directions, which are always given from a place of love, because *'God is love'!* (1 John 4:8)

Therefore, by following Christ, we cannot merely ask Him into our lives and then follow our inclinations. The world's way and Jesus' way are two very different paths (Matthew 7:13-14).

The Cost of Loving Jesus

For myself, the cost of following Jesus has meant that I have lost relationships with family members and even friends, dreams that I wanted in life (before coming a Christian), and truthfully, even the love of being materialistic.

I used to love the 'finer things in life'. My parents were working-class, and we didn't have a lot of money growing up; but my brother and I never went without, as our parents sought to provide for us.

As a child we never think about the bigger picture; and looking back, I was only concerned with the latest trends and what my friends were doing. Whereas now, although I still like nice things,

I place less value on materialistic items and more on what God wants me to do.

When God's way conflicts with our own, we can tend to feel hurt by what we believed God would do for us. It's like being a child all over again with the 'What about me'? attitude.

We lead lives of false faith-based practices that tend to crumble when things get tough because our faith isn't based on the Word of God but more on 'What can God do for us'?

The 'Me first' faith doesn't count the cost of being God's child; therefore, when we feel the burden to give something up, we will turn away from Christ rather than our desires to be fulfilled.

Jesus has become *just our Saviour,* not the Lord and Saviour of our lives (Romans 10). Those with a 'Me first' faith is what I see as the 'sleeping church', as written about in Revelation 3:1-3. These Christians love the idea of following Jesus, but because there is no real requirement of what a Christian is supposed to do within the Bible, compared to the requirements of being a disciple, therefore, they feel that living a life that 'doesn't hurt anyone' will result in eternal living. But *we cannot just live a life based on those basic principles,* as this is called 'cheap grace'.

Just Believing Isn't Enough

Cheap grace hides the cost of true discipleship from people since it states that as long as we say that we believe in Christ, we are saved. God's grace *does cover all of our sins,* that is a biblical truth—but the apostle Paul reiterates my point when he writes:

> *'Just as sin reigned in death, so also grace might reign through righteousness to bring eternal life through Jesus Christ our Lord. Well then, should we keep on sinning so that God can show us more and more of his wonderful grace? Of course not! Since we have died to sin, how can we continue to live in it'?*
> Romans 5:21-6:2

Paul was saying that salvation is so much more than just mouthing the words, 'Jesus is Lord'. That means that just praying the sinners' prayer or signing a card at the church or a conference does not save us. We are, however, saved by a living and active faith (James 2:14-26), a faith that manifests itself in repentance, obedience, a love for God, and a love for our neighbours. Salvation is not just a transaction; it's a transformation.[2]

> **'What a heartbreak it would be to live an "almost" Christian life, then "almost" get into Heaven'.**
> *Greg Laurie*

Life won't remain the same if Jesus is in charge.

When we become Jesus' disciples, when we choose to follow Him, or when we choose to release the power over our lives and let Jesus have full control, we become more Christlike, and that's the transformation. The outworking of discipleship is evident to see because we are never the same again.

In my life the cursing stopped, the need to drink alcohol regularly was gone, and wanting to be in a nightclub every week ceased. Life was no longer about me. My thoughts had turned to Jesus, and the things that I felt were important before, now seemed insignificant.

Some of Jesus' disciples in this world have lost their lives (or loved ones) because they followed Him and even ten out of the eleven apostles were killed for their faith.

The organisation Open Doors USA states that there are currently 322 Christians worldwide being killed each month because of their Christian faith.[3] These people, just like the apostles, would not denounce Christ, so they are murdered for that simple reason.

Don't misunderstand me. I am not saying that being a disciple means that we have to die for our faith, but there is a vast difference between people who call themselves Christians, and those who follow all of Jesus' ways; no matter the sacrifice or cost to themselves.

What Is a Disciple?

Mathētēs is the Greek word for student, pupil, or even learner; but in ancient Greek, the translation would be seen more like someone who was *devoted* to his or her teacher. That's a big difference! In other words, the teacher's ways become your ways.

Discipleship should, therefore, bring the same sort of thought processes to Christians, in such a way that we become devoted to Jesus. In other words, we become faithful and loyal to His teachings.

When Jesus said to 'make disciples' it was for Christians to bring people who do not know God into a relationship with Him, through Christ. But our Teacher, Jesus, then showed us that it is not merely just about leading people to accept Him into their lives, as mentioned, because Jesus ensured that *He* spent time with the Father through prayer and He *also* read the Scriptures diligently *and then* taught them to His followers to encourage, uplift, and build their faith.

When Jesus did this, He was able to build trust over the three years He taught His disciples, by showing that He was who He proclaimed to be and ultimately, the prophecies that He was to fulfil.

This faith and trust that Jesus built were then evident; because people will not die for a cause they don't believe in, regardless of their belief system, faith, religion, or cause they are fighting for.

CHAPTER TWO

HOW DO WE BECOME DISCIPLES?

How Can We Bear Fruit?

'Salvation is free, but discipleship will cost you your life'.
Dietrich Bonhoeffer

1. Build our relationship with God.

Jesus said:

> *'You are truly my disciples if you remain faithful to my teachings. And you will know the truth, and the truth will set you free'.* John 8:31-32

In John 15:1-4, Jesus tells us what we need to do to be able to remain faithful to His teachings, as a disciple of His. There are certain things necessary for this to be accomplished but this is where Jesus talks about vines.

He reminds the disciples that to be His means to bear fruit, and we do this by remaining in Him.

Jesus describes Himself as:

'the true grapevine, and my Father is the gardener'. John 15:1

The disciples would have understood what Jesus was saying because they would have grown up learning the Torah. But for us, Jesus was talking about the vineyard that Isaiah had prophesied about, in chapter 5 of Isaiah's book.

The vine that Isaiah talked about was a symbol of Israel: a nation that God carefully 'planted' in the Promised Land. God had looked after their every need, but He only found 'bad fruit'.

Therefore, when Jesus said to the disciples that He was the true vine, He was saying that He was the genuine Israel, who will produce the fruit of goodness and love. Jesus was reiterating to them that He is the Messiah; and consequently, the fulfilment of the prophecy given to us by Isaiah.

Jesus is always intentional with the parables and pictures He spoke about, and the vine demonstrates humility on our part—that's why Jesus chose this because it's a picture of a permanent and fundamental union between the vine and branches.

The branches belong entirely to the vine and therefore are symbolic; if they are to live and bear fruit (as designed to do), then they must entirely depend on the vine for their sustenance, strength, and livelihood.

How many of us fail to depend entirely on Christ? Instead of being connected to the 'true vine' for life, we have our income, education, popularity, possessions, or worldly desires. Nothing except Christ, who is the true vine—can sustain us or allow us to bear fruit that God ultimately wants from us.

So, looking at the passage in John 15, Jesus explains in more detail what the vines and branches mean. They are those who are followers of Christ. Now remember, there's a difference between being a follower and claiming to be a follower.

The fruitful branches are His believers who produce fruit (think 'Fruit of the Spirit') and they do so by remaining connected to the vine.

It is a beautiful picture of God's love at work in our lives because Jesus gives life to us, just as the vine pours life into its fruit. The vine and the branch are connected and maintain that relationship.

Distinctions

Jesus then goes on to use a distinction between two kinds of pruning branches: cutting back branches and separating.

Even fruitful branches are cut back to promote growth. God does this to purify, encourage, and bring correction in the areas that are needed. This then bears more fruit in our lives.

The description of fruit merely is a symbol of our Christian character and faith, because the Bible says that to grow in nature, we need to become more like Christ. We must decrease our fleshly desires for Christ to increase in our lives. (John 3:30)

I am someone who loves all types of plants. However, just because I love them does not make me qualified in knowing what is best for them.

I have been known to kill plants, unintentionally I hasten to add. I have also been known to kill a cactus. Yes, they can die, and I know you may laugh! However, the irony is that either I forgot to water the plants or in the case of the cactus I overwatered it!

Even though I tried to care for them as much as possible, I often fail miserably. Death happens over a period of time; the plant is unable to obtain the nourishment needed and therefore it withers and dies from wrong nutrition.

The same thing for living out our Christian lives; if we are not getting the right nourishment, then eventually our faith can wither and die.

Don't Be a Judas

When Jesus was talking about the vine, it was during the last supper with His disciples. Jesus had already been aware of the difference between Judas and the other disciples. After washing their feet, Jesus replied:

> 'Those who have had a bath need only to wash their feet; their whole body is clean. And you are clean, though not every one of you'. John 13:10-11 NIV

Once God forgives a Christian and Christ is in their heart *as Lord and Saviour,* they are clean and right before God; therefore, that person does not need to be continually bathed, which is symbolic of baptism, for forgiveness.

All Jesus was saying was from that point onwards is to clean the dust and dirt from the daily sins of life off our feet. We do not need to be continually saved again and again, but rather that we need to restore our relationship with God through prayer, reading the Word, and being led by the Spirit.

Jesus knew that there was a difference between His disciples and that's why He added: *'not all of you'* were clean because although Judas appeared to be like all the other disciples, and he was even with Jesus for the same amount of time as the others—learning and listening to Jesus' teachings—there was a vast difference.

It appeared to everyone else that Judas was a branch in the vine, like all of the other disciples; and although Peter denied Christ, he came to Christ in repentance, which Jesus then restored and built His church upon. (Matthew 16:18) Whereas, Judas took his own life. (Matthew 27:5)

Do you find it fascinating that the one thing that Judas had been given the responsibility for (money) was the one thing that ultimately led to his destruction? Sometimes the very things that we are given to steward in this world are the very things that will eventually tear us down because we do it in our own strength instead of giving it back to God and serving under Him.

Giving Our Decisions to God

David said:

> *'Give your burdens to the Lord, and he will take care of you...'.* Psalm 55:22

But there are two parts to that verse; the second part is:

> *'...He will not permit the godly to slip and fall'.* Psalm 55:22

Even at a moment when we are slipping, God is still gracious enough to hold us. Hence why, when God is with us and we walk with Him, we will not fall! (Psalm 46:5 NIV)

Yes, I know there can be times when we can make decisions that are outside of God's plan for our lives, but when we turn back to Christ, He will hold us up. Helping us not to fall into our enemies' hands, as we trust that when we ask for forgiveness, we will be forgiven.

Jesus made a promise to His children, and it's the same today as it was then, He said:

> *'I give them eternal life, and they will never perish. No one can snatch them away from me'.* John 10:28

Unfortunately, although this is a controversial topic, the Bible shows us that we can lose our salvation because of our worldly desires, and the need to follow our flesh rather than God's direction. This then draws us away from Him over time.

> *'Dear friends, if we deliberately continue sinning after we have received knowledge of the truth, there is no longer any sacrifice that will cover these sins'.* Hebrews 10:26

'The Four Soils' found in Mark 4:1-20 is a great parable to represent four different ways that people can respond to God's message. Jesus explains the responses we can have towards the Gospel, but ultimately someone who is genuinely saved by God's grace will show this by it out-working in the person's life.

But with regards to when Jesus is talking about the vines being separated, if you look at what the apostle Paul speaks about in Galatians 5:22-23, there are specific characteristics that God has given. When they are evident in our lives, those characteristics, or the Fruit of the Spirit, naturally draw others to us by seeing the Christlike attributes in our personality. Real branches develop those features or 'bear fruit'—always!

Therefore, just as we know when a healthy tree produces good fruit, so can we also recognise fruitless branches having no fruit and Jesus tells us:

> 'You can identify them, by their fruit, that is, by the way, they act.... So every tree that does not produce good fruit is chopped down and thrown into the fire'. Matthew 7:16,19

The reference in verse 19 is for those who abandon their faith, or they are in a relationship with Christ that is insincere. Eventually, the Bible shows us that these branches as identified as not belonging to the vine are removed for the sake of the other branches and the truth of God.

Now, this isn't for anyone of us to say that our family, friends, or acquaintances aren't Christians. That's not how it works. If God is the only one who can see a person's real heart, then we are not to judge anyone by his or her actions, whether seemingly Christian or not, and God will judge all of us, at the right time, according to His perfect will.

Intimacy with God

Having an intimate relationship with God and walking with the Spirit every day would mean that we are not seeking what this world has to offer because we understand that this is only temporary; but also, we then become obedient to God's Word, enabling us to stay connected to the true vine.

That is when our character will start to be transformed and produce 'good fruit'. Jesus is, after all, the Living Word of God; and when Jesus taught His disciples the Scriptures, it was because obeying the Word of God is also conforming to Jesus Christ (John 1:1).

2. Prayer[4]

Jesus taught us how to come to God through the Lord's Prayer in the Gospel of Matthew. This prayer shouldn't necessarily be recited over and over as it is more of a guide, but God is far more interested in our hearts behind the prayer, rather than what we say or how we say it.

Therefore, I want us to look at the Lord's Prayer as the fundamental piece of how we should formulate our prayers because it will help us to become more intimate with God (Matthew 6:9-13 NIV):

"Our Father in heaven."
- This phrase teaches us to address all of our prayers to the Father.
- It's a loving invitation to pray as a member of God's family because we are adopted as a son or daughter of the Living God. Jesus invites us to address His Father as our Father too.

"Hallowed be Your Name."
- This phrase tells us to worship God and praise Him for what He has done.
- Psalm 91:1-2 is known as the psalm of protection, and it shows us just a few of the names God is known by:
    - The Most High (El Elyon, which means He has no equal)
    - The Almighty (El Shaddai, which means, the God who is more than enough). The LORD (Jehovah, which means, I AM)
    - My God (Elohim, which means, God or Creator)

The Lord's Prayer is such a beautiful piece of Scripture, and whatever we are going through, we can use God's name in power because of who He is.

'Your kingdom come, Your will be done, on earth as it is in heaven'.
- This verse reminds us that we need to pray for God's will in our lives and the world. It's not for our desires or plans, but His.
- It's a reminder that we need to take back the sense of "being out of control" in our lives because we carry the authority of Christ.

- Everything comes under God's reign, and therefore we need to pray for our lives, family, church, and nation.
- If God's will comes, then the Kingdom of Heaven comes with Him to Earth.
- The fruits of His Kingdom manifest as…
  - People will be saved (2 Peter 3:9)
  - The bound will be set free (Luke 4:18-19)
  - The sick will be healed (Matthew 10:1)
- Our souls will prosper, amongst other things (3 John 2)
- Prayer, thanksgiving, rejoicing (1 Thessalonians 5:16-18)

'Give us today our daily bread'.
- This verse encourages us to ask for things that we need.
- God has provided everything we need (Philippians 4:12)

Please let me explain 'daily bread'. It isn't about prosperity as such, but teaching what Paul says in Philippians 4:12; we need to have balance. I believe there are four things we can do to obtain what we need and rightfully pray to God:
1. Be in God's will (surrender and be in fellowship with Him)
2. Fellowship within the local church (not just attend)
3. Developing a balance and discipline with work and hobbies
4. Being faithful in our giving of tithes and offerings!

How do we receive our daily bread?
- Believe when you pray in faith to God that you will receive.
- Be specific. Ask specifically for what you need for yourself, your family, and for others, as well as for your church and its outreaches.
- Do NOT give up! (Read Luke 18 – The Persistent Widow)

'And forgive us our debts, as we also have forgiven our debtors'.
- This verse reminds us to confess any sins to God and turn away from them but also to forgive others as God forgives us.

It was after this prayer that Jesus emphasises the importance of forgiveness again. Could it be we need to be reminded? (Matthew 18:21-22).

'And lead us not into temptation, but deliver us from the evil one'.
- This last verse is a plea to help us to achieve victory over sin in our lives and request protection from the attacks of the enemy.
- God can teach us through temptation, but His plan will always be for us to learn the correct way because Scripture and the Holy Spirit should bring correction, not the devil and his temptations.
- This part of Scripture gives us a fantastic insight into how we should approach prayer and talk with God.

I would not say I am an 'expert' in prayer, but my prayer life has grown over the years as I continue to walk with God. My one-way demands have become a two-way conversation.

My requests have become more about seeking God's will for my circumstances, and that means trusting the process that God takes me through rather than trying to control each move I make.
- Prayer is talking to God and getting to know Him and His heart for my life, through His voice.
- We need to be listening for His voice, and that can happen in various ways. It is normal for you to be able to hear from

God and He definitely wants to communicate with us all, but sometimes we can miss out on hearing Him because we don't know how He speaks.
- From time to time we can wander from God like sheep, walking without a Shepherd, thus without direction at all, but John 10:27 (NKJV) says:

'My sheep hear My voice, and I know them, and they follow Me'.

How Can We Hear God's Voice?

If you think about this question, most of the time we immediately focus on God's audible voice; and yes, God can speak to us that way, but God treats us all differently and what may be a 'normal' way for you to hear God, may look different to the next person.

He doesn't speak the same way to all of us. However, there are specific ways that God uses to communicate, and I want to go through some of them.

Now I know that this is not an exhaustive list, but when we start to understand this concept, we can begin to be led by God in ways that we had never considered before:

God Speaks through the Bible

The original Greek language uses two different words for 'Word':

Logos, which is the written Word as we have it today called the Bible.

Rhema, which is the Voice we hear from the Holy Spirit, and it's where the words within the Bible become 'alive' to us.

How Do We Become Disciples?

Faith is activated when we hear or feel a message through our spirit by reading the Bible (Romans 10:17 NIV) and, unless a person hears God's voice or perceives it through their spirit, the Bible will always remain *logos,* or just words on a page, because there will be no *rhema:*

'For we live by believing and not by seeing'. 2 Corinthians 5:7

God uses the Bible to speak to us, and He confirms this when we can see what He has done before, in the lives of so many other people in Scripture, then we have the confidence that no matter what is happening to us, God can deliver us as He delivered them within the Bible stories. Therefore, in studying and learning these stories, it creates faith in us to continue on and see God's deliverance for our own lives.

We should spend time reading the Bible every day because God can prepare our hearts to receive His truth from Scripture. The words become alive with meaning, and that brings revelation into our spirits: this is the *Rhema* Word.

God also speaks to us about the situations we are facing each day through the Scriptures, which He wrote through people thousands of years ago! I find this amazing, as we want God to 'speak to us' but we don't take the time to find out what He has already spoken through the Bible.

The Word of God is as active and alive today (Hebrews 4:12 NIV), as it was when it was first written, because:

'All Scripture is God-breathed…'. 2 Timothy 3:16 NIV

I can remember the first time that God spoke to me through the Bible. It was late at night, and I was reading Romans 8, which is 'Life Through the Spirit'.

I was so excited because I felt as if God was talking directly to me and those words had been written in preparation for Rebecca Brand with what was to come in my life! So I woke up Kieren, my husband, to go through what had just happened. He tried to be enthusiastic for me but there and then, I alone, developed a hunger for God's Word.

God Can Speak to You through Other Christians

Again, don't misunderstand me, it doesn't mean that we should accept everything we hear from friends, parents, mentors, or even a preacher as a 'word from God'. Generally, however, if we are receiving the same message over and over from various sources, then it could be that God *is* confirming His word by repetition.

Most importantly, whether we choose to hear the words or ignore them depends entirely on us, yet we must ensure the words line up with Scripture:

> *'But the wisdom from above is first of all pure. It is also peace loving, gentle at all times, and willing to yield to others. It is full of mercy and the fruit of good deeds. It shows no favouritism and is always sincere'.* James 3:17 ESV

And, if we haven't heard a message before, then ask God to confirm the word. Pray, because we can tend to box God in with the ways we think He will speak to us; but if God can use a donkey to talk to a person (Numbers 22:28), then He can certainly use other people.

God Speaks through Music

One of my favourite ways to hear God's voice is through music. The words go deep into my soul and no matter what my circumstance at that time, I sense God's presence when I'm praising Him.

I joke to my family that I can live without TV, DVDs, cinema, etc., but I couldn't live without music. I am always listening to praise or worship or even singing to myself, because the words I hear bring joy or comfort to me. I always think of the angels and the elders singing before the throne along with every Christian worshipping God:

> *'And all the angels were standing around the throne and around the elders and the four living beings. And they fell before the throne with their faces to the ground and worshipped God'.*
> Revelation 7:11

Can you imagine the sound that comes from the world every day from Christians praising God, along with those in Heaven? We were created to worship, and so it makes sense that God will speak to us through music as well.

God Will Also Lead Us by the Holy Spirit

Within the New Testament, it shows that God will also lead us by the Holy Spirit time after time again. However, when we say that the Spirit doesn't lead us, then the issue could honestly be that we are too inflexible (or can I say stubborn in our ways) with wanting to understand, because we don't want to really discover God's will for our lives!

It may seem too hard, or we might even feel we are having too much fun in the worldly ways to change; but I want you to note that God does not reveal His truth to those who are not willing to surrender to Jesus.

Jesus needs to be Lord in our lives and not just our Saviour. Paul tells us:

> *'Don't copy the behaviour and customs of this world, but let God transform you into a new person by changing the way you think, then you will learn to know God's will for your life, which is good and pleasing and perfect'.* Romans 12:2

When I spoke about reading Romans 8 in the Bible; from that day, I mentioned that I had a hunger for God's Word, but it was more than that. From that moment, I wanted to know God intimately and His purposes for my life. I desired to depend on the Spirit to give me direction.

It blows my mind that those who will read this book, each one will walk away with a different truth that will apply to their life. This is another example of *Rhema,* because people 'hear' a living truth into their spirits, from God's Spirit.

Scripture again comes alive because it becomes personal to the individual.

The most direct way God speaks to us is through a small still voice.

I hope that you are beginning to understand that God is not going to only talk to us with a booming voice from the sky, like in the movies! But He can speak to us in a whisper. So, how do we hear a whisper? By making sure God's voice is the loudest voice in our life.

I love the Scripture in 1 Kings 19:11-12, where Elijah witnesses a great wind, earthquake and then a fire, but he ultimately, after all of those events have occurred, finds God in a gentle whisper.

God does not need to yell when He speaks to us to get our attention. His voice is like a whisper deep within.

Elijah knew that he was in the presence of the Lord, but when God speaks, unfortunately, it can be all too easy to ignore. The Holy Spirit is a 'gentleman', and God is not about forcing us to obey what He said to us, because that takes away from the purpose of free will.

I think we can learn a lot from this passage in 1 Kings.

God can be dramatic and spectacular, and this was the case with what Elijah witnessed in his 'mountaintop experience' at Mount Carmel. Elijah had just challenged all the false prophets of Baal to a contest, and God demonstrated His power that day. (1 Kings 18)

But, as Israel came to acknowledge the Lord once more, Elijah had gone from being victorious in putting to death the prophets, to being afraid, entering into a period of depression, and having wavering faith because he was running for his own life from Queen Jezebel. Elijah fled to the wilderness and even prayed for God to take his life! His soul had gone from standing on the mount with God, to running into the valley of suicide.

Most often, God's divine purposes for our lives are carried to us by gentle whispers, when He speaks to our very hearts.

God is so relatable to us in an intimate and personal manner; and by communicating to Elijah this way, it shows us that we can be mighty for God when we are attentive to His voice.

Like King David, we need to seek God:

> *'O God, you are my God; I earnestly search for you. My soul thirsts for you; my whole body longs for you in this parched and weary land where there is no water'.* Psalm 63:1

We need to be open and honest with where we actually are in life and earnestly seek the difference between God's gentle voice and our thoughts.

We need to be good listeners and not try to listen to God when the TV's on, or the kids are screaming at each other! We need to be intentional and make time for God in this crazily busy world!

I love that God asked Elijah to stand on the mountain as He passed by; because when Elijah was obedient and still, that is when he heard from the Lord.

Desiring God Above All Else

I wanted to give you a taste of how God speaks because I want us to desire to become disciples of Christ.

After all, that is the purpose that God desires for us: that we will follow His ways, His guidance, and listen for His voice. God wants to partner with us and, who knows, perhaps we *were made* for such a time as this! (Esther 4:14)

An analogy of this is found when Jesus told the disciples about the parable of the sower; it was only the soil that allowed the seed to put down roots and bear fruit that was called 'good' (Luke 8:1-15).

> *'Every Christian is either a missionary or an imposter'.*
> **Charles Spurgeon**

Evangelism is One of the Keys

With this in mind, just as the disciples were told to spread the gospel, our ultimate purpose is the same. Evangelism is bringing others into a relationship with God, through Jesus Christ.

I remember very clearly saying that I am not an evangelist. The dreaded "E" word used to fill me with fear and even anger, and yet the great commission shows that we are *all called to evangelise.*

So with all of our different personalities, talents, and backgrounds, why not allow God to show us how to use our God-given gifts to reach others in this messed-up world?

There are six distinct styles of evangelism within the Bible. The following list has been adapted from *Becoming a Courageous Christian* by Bill Hybels and Mark Mittelberg.

Therefore, as we read over them, we need to ask ourselves if one or more might fit with who we are as individuals.[5] I won't expand further on these styles because ultimately, this isn't the purpose of this book, but it is one of the keys to unlocking how we might feel more comfortable with speaking about Jesus to others in our lives!

Direct Style
- Biblical example: Peter (Acts 2)
- Characteristics: confident, undeviating, bold, and assertive.
- Theme verse: 2 Timothy 4:2
- Be careful not to offend people and be sure to use tact.

Intellectual Style
- Biblical example: Paul (Acts 17)
- Characteristics: analytical, logical and inquisitive.
- Theme verse: 1 Peter 3:15
- Be careful not to become argumentative and forget to share the Gospel! Remember to listen to others as well.

Testimonial Style
- Biblical example: Blind man (John 9)
- Characteristics: faithful and humble (always glorifies God).
- Theme verse: 1 John 1:3
- Be careful not to only talk about yourself but remember to tell people about what Jesus has done for you.

Interpersonal Style
- Biblical example: Matthew (Luke 5:29)
- Characteristics: conversational, friendly, people-focused.
- Theme verse: 1 Corinthians 9:22
- Be careful not to value friendships or relationships over telling the truth.

Invitational Style

- Biblical example: The Samaritan Woman (John 4)
- Characteristics: hospitable, relational and persuasive
- Theme verse: Luke 14:23
- There are no cautions, as merely giving an invitation to someone can change their life!

Serving Style

- Biblical example: Dorcas (Acts 9:36)
- Characteristics: self-less, humble, patient and caring
- Theme verse: Matthew 5:16
- Be careful not to substitute words with actions – Romans 10:14.

God built diversity within the body of Christ for a reason. Therefore, we need to stop imitating each other and, I believe, stop squashing each other's creativity, because we not only seem to want to box believers in but ultimately God as well.

Can you imagine what would happen if every Christian would evangelise openly?

For instance, if every person had the mindset that the people they shared the gospel with would come to Christ, would we then become excited about sharing our faith, if you knew there was no risk of rejection involved?

We cannot control if the person we talk to about Christ rejects God, because free will is just that; they need to accept Christ into their hearts freely. Paul says:

'Satan, who is the god of this world, has blinded the minds of those who don't believe. They are unable to see the glorious light of the Good News…'. 2 Corinthians 4:4

Therefore, we shouldn't be discouraged, as mentioned at the start of this chapter, because God wants *everyone* to be in heaven with Him. But it will be the free will of those individuals who trusted in themselves more than Christ that determines whether they spend eternity with Christ or not.

Our purpose is to complete the task that Jesus has given for us, as the whole body of Christ, which is to fulfil the great commission. It doesn't say that we are to present the gospel to all people but all people groups, and it is also not our job to convince those people that God is real because God is big enough to do that on His own.

CHAPTER THREE

DOES GOD ACTUALLY EXIST?

How Can You Be Sure When You Can't Actually See Him?

> *'Heaven is real and hell is real, and*
> *eternity is but a breath away'.*
> **Billy Graham**

Faith in the Unseen

As an individual who has gone from atheism to Christianity, I now know that it takes more faith to not believe in God than it does to believe in Him.

Therefore, this was the fundamental reason that I felt the need to write this chapter because of what I witnessed while I was still an atheist. To be honest, there wasn't one person, at the time, who I could honestly say gave me an answer that made me think differently about my mindset.

Now you might feel that I was probably confident in my belief system, or maybe I had a strong personality in that I could give a compelling argument, no matter what the topic, yet the Bible is clear:

> *'...And if someone asks about your hope as a believer, always be ready to explain it. But do this in a gentle and respectful way. Keep your conscience clear. Then if people speak against you, they will be ashamed when they see what a good life you live because you belong to Christ'.* 1 Peter 3:15-16

Being sincere, I am not very good at arguing, as I get tongue-tied and my brain and mouth seem to lose cohesion!

I find that most of the time our emotions can get the better of us, and I have experienced that it can simply become a slanging match between different parties.

I love Christian apologetics; because there are so many false doctrines and people who deny the fundamentals of the Christian faith, an apologist seeks to combat these movements and promote the only true faith by defending God's Word.

Believers should know what they believe in and why they think it. Peter confirms this; but people should also know how to share their faith (as I discussed in the last chapter regarding evangelism). And lastly, people should be comfortable with how to defend those beliefs against the lies and attacks of others!

Three Important Questions
1. What do you believe?
2. How did God become alive to you?
3. How did He reveal Himself to you?

If you are a Christian, then these questions might seem irrelevant. The most common answer I would hear when challenging Christians was, 'Because I do'. Therefore, as an atheist, I found it easy to take people away from their faith!

'Because I do', never brings honour to God or even defends our beliefs; and so I was able to pull apart the frailty of that individual's viewpoint. If we do not know what we believe, how are we supposed to tell someone else?

You could be reading this book and have known God for years, and yet you still have questions about who God is, but you don't want to ask anyone.

Maybe you do not know who Christ is at all, and you picked up this book, intrigued; but whatever category you fit into, these three questions, can change your life forever. Why? Because if we allow it, they will get us thinking, and the Bible commands that we seek knowledge, gain understanding, and get wisdom—because we don't know what we don't know.

'Get wisdom, get understanding; do not forget my words or turn away from them'. Proverbs 4:5 NIV

Ultimately, I want us to consider these arguments that I discuss for the rest of the chapter. I am not writing about the arguments to convince you, because I could write a book in itself on these topics, but I desire that we start to think for ourselves about the world and how we perceive it, along with what God says about them.

Brainwashed

As a child we generally take on the belief system of our parents. For me that meant atheism; and honestly, I didn't have any thoughts that would lead me to doubt what my parents had taught me.

I remember my dad would tell me that atheism made sense only because 'Christian-freaks' had been brainwashed. After all, if there were a God then surely He would stop things like wars, famine, murder, and natural disasters, to name a few.

So, I became bitter and angry at the thought of the stupid and naïve people in this world. I mean, how could so many people not know that this God was making a fool out of them?

Looking back now, to say a Christian is brainwashed is the same as saying that I was conditioned to my parent's belief system. It means that everyone in the world is conditioned in one way or another.

My family believes there is no God because of the pain in this world, but atheism is a belief system, based on a belief alone, just like most religions.

In other words, we had no faith in God, but our faith and trust were in the belief that there was no God, because of the suffering we see worldwide. I have realised that it is just a question of whether others have the same viewpoint.

At around twenty-five years old, I remember thinking that rather than imagining there was no God (because He was outside of the framework of my thinking), I wanted to try and prove why I believed that there was, in fact, no God. I love to discuss with people their viewpoints on life, and I wanted to say more than 'Because I don't' if asked a specific question.

I went on a journey, as we all do in some way during life, and I found God. Plus, He showed me that He is more real than I could have ever imagined! I couldn't 'see' Him previously. I now know that just because you cannot see the wind does not mean that it's not there. The same applies to God.

Start Asking Questions
At some point in our lives, we need to start asking questions. I don't have a gift as an apologist,[6] but I think that this topic can be one of the most significant battles that we can face in life. Therefore, I believe it is imperative to briefly ask the question again, as some people still struggle to think about it:

Is God real? I think that it is a valid question!

All of the nations around the world will get the chance to hear the gospel at some point. After all, in the book of Matthew it says:

> *'And the Good News about the Kingdom will be preached throughout the whole world, so that all nations will hear it, and then the end will come'.* Matthew 24:14

But once your heart is open to God, as a Christian, do we have the faith and trust in Him to believe in who He says He is?

There are countless stories of people walking away from their faith, since from the time that Jesus died on the cross until this very day. Timothy warned us of this in the Bible:

> *'The Holy Spirit has explicitly revealed: At the end of this age, many will depart from the true faith one after another, devoting themselves to spirits of deception and following demon-inspired revelations and theories'.* 1 Timothy 4:1 TPT

Timothy was saying that some will fall away from Christ, as they believe the enemy rather than the Word of God. So, let me ask:
- What do you believe?
- How do you know that God is real?

These are good questions to ask yourself; and as we have discovered, the Bible is clear that we should be ready to give an account when asked. (1 Peter 3:15)

Therefore, for the rest of this chapter, I want to go through the 'arguments for the existence of God'.[7]

What I write is neither an exhaustive list nor every detail on each of the arguments, but I also want to reiterate, that I am not trying to persuade you of anything because you are on your journey just like me, so think of this as an introductory guide.

I have found these arguments to be invaluable over the last few years to cement my belief system and the fundamentals of my faith because these arguments have shown me who God is from a philosophical or logical viewpoint; but most importantly, I am now always ready to answer these questions.

I love to be able to look at an argument that is given and then go away and search for an answer from a rational standpoint that I agree with.

Everyone has some sort of opinion towards God, but I feel researching the answers ourselves, and then testing it against Scripture is the best way, because eventually we will all give an account to God, individually. (Romans 14:12)

> *'The devil doesn't know what to do with*
> *somebody who just won't give up'*
> *Joyce Meyer*

The Cosmological Argument

In Greek, *cosmos* means 'world'. Therefore, this argument looks at the world and then speaks on cause and effect, which is the relationship between events, where one is the result of the other. For example, if I flicked on a light switch, the light would come on.

Many amazing people over the centuries have debated the fact that the world is even here. They have asked numerous times, "Why is there something rather than nothing?" Now there is a question!

The majority of scientists today confirm the cosmological argument to be true because of thermodynamics. I want to try and keep this as simple as possible, but there are two laws of thermodynamics. The first law is: mass-energy can neither be created nor destroyed. Robert Mayer (1814-1878) initially gave this formulation, but this law has never been disproved, so to develop a concept against this would go against scientific evidence. The first law leads to the universe existing eternally.[8] In other words, the universe and everything in it will exist in one form or another—forever.

However, Dr Robert Gange who wrote *Origins and Destiny*, noted, 'The older idea of an eternally existing world is now known to have a problem...that it had a beginning'.[9] This statement is because of the second law of thermodynamics, which is: the amount of energy available...is running out.

So, how can the universe, which is supposedly eternal (first law), be running out of energy (second law)? Fascinating isn't it!

This argument seems sensible to me because the universe needs to have a beginning (cause) to coincide with the second law.

God, on the other hand, has no beginning because He is eternal. (Deuteronomy 33:27) He is the Creator of the whole universe, including time (Genesis 1:1), so exists outside of it and therefore doesn't need a cause, because He is not created.

The apostle Paul gives a fantastic insight into trusting in the existence of God in the book of Acts. He says:

> *'He is the God who made the world and everything in it. Since he is Lord of heaven and earth, he doesn't live in man-made temples, and human hands can't serve his needs—for he has no needs. He himself gives life and breath to everything, and he satisfies every need'.* Acts 17:24-25

The Teleological Argument

The word *telos* means 'purpose' in Greek, so this argument looks at the world from this perspective. Meaning everything has a perfect design that was created with a purpose and not just by chance.

For instance, there are things in the world that are in harmony and science cannot explain them. For example:

- Each snowflake is different and yet a perfect design.
- The earth is at the right distance from the sun to receive the proper amounts of heat and light for photosynthesis to occur.
- The sea is at just the right salt level to sustain life.
- The earth's distance from the sun is crucial for a stable water cycle, and this is perfect. Too close, we'd boil. Too far, we'd freeze.
- The earth's gravity, axial tilt, rotation, ozone level, and much more are all 'just right'.

I find it hard to believe that any of these things could happen by chance, and this was something I struggled with before I found God. I wanted to know why things were perfect in design, and why science could not explain them. Therefore, the more time I spend on this earth, the more illogical it seems not to be able to see a Creator.

I love what philosopher Norman Geisler concludes: 'There may be some theoretical chance that wind and rain erosion could produce the faces of four presidents on the side of a mountain, but it is still far more reasonable to assume that an intelligent sculptor created Mount Rushmore'.[10]

With this in mind, a perfectly designed universe points to someone who is far more, infinitely more, intelligent than you or I can comprehend.

> *'In him lie hidden all the treasures of wisdom and knowledge'.*
> Colossians 2:3

God is omniscient, which means that He has total knowledge of everything! He is all-knowing. And although this is just one of His attributes, we need to try and realise that we cannot understand everything because we are limited; whereas, God is not.

There could even be more to God's character, but we only know what He has revealed to us through Scripture; and even then, we are limited to perceiving Him through our senses. We understand the world and even God by sight, hearing, touch, taste, smell. Although our understanding of Him might be correct, it will not be complete!

Regardless of whether we understand this concept or not, the evidence is clear to see that there must be a living God who is our Creator and Designer. (Romans 1:20)

My dad is one who always likes to state that unless he can see God, he will never believe in Him. While this might be compelling within my father's thoughts, it always amazes me that people, like my dad, have more belief in things such as a watchmaker did in fact make their watch. Or that a pilot is flying a plane; or maybe that a chair will take their weight, then they have in their ability to believe in God.

This argument shows that everything has its place; it works in unison together and cannot be an accident.

The Anthropological Argument
This argument goes through the study of humankind (Greek *anthropos*) and why we are so different from other forms of life on this planet.

We are God's masterpiece because we were made in His image to be the glory of creation. (Genesis 1:27) In other words, we cannot come from an ape or a fish because we are far superior to all of the other animals within the world we live in; and more importantly, there is no proof of it occurring. If there were, inevitably we would have fossil evidence to show the transitional species between humans and whatever species we have come from.

Palaeontologists have not found intermediate species in the fossils of birds, animals, or even mammals, and there is an absence to show another species turning into a human, i.e., a fish into a man.

Just a side note, but you would have thought that from the billions of people who have died there would be at least a few fossils to prove the macroevolutionary theories?

I believe that human beings are all distinct and unique and therefore strongly bear the mark of creatorship upon them. Some people say that Christians do not believe in evolution, but I disagree with this statement.

I do not believe in macroevolution because there is no evidence to prove it. However with microevolution, there's proof of individual traits changing over time within a population of species. For example, cats have evolved, see Pseudaelurus, and we can see the evolutionary inherited traits that have taken place.

In the book of Genesis it says:

> 'God made all sorts of wild animals, livestock, and small animals, each able to produce offspring of the same kind...'.
> Genesis 1:25

This Scripture is referring to creating animals according to their kind, which again reconfirms the microevolution theory, as mentioned.

The Moral Argument

This argument comes from the basis that humanity possesses an inner sense of what is right and wrong; but more than that, we have a responsibility to adhere to that code. The Bible labels this as a 'conscience', and it is God-given. (Romans 2:14-15)

Have you ever thought about the fact that those living within Western society do not live without some moral law?

Everyday life sees the likes of the police, solicitors, medical professionals, and even ordinary citizens standing for justice and human rights. We see a snapshot of this within the media, but whether the reports are correct or not, we all have a viewpoint on the things occurring locally, nationally, or even globally.

We argue over what is right or wrong. We condemn the actions of rape, murder, violence, child abuse, war, and racism, to name a small few, but then we see the people convicted as evil or wrong within our moral and ethically based universe.

Who gets to decide or dictate what perspective is correct?

Different countries see moral and ethical standards differently. For instance, what might be deemed as barbaric to Western society—individuals being stoned to death—in other societies is seen as merely doing what is expected.

However, for humanity to say that something, or someone, is right or wrong requires a higher standard of living. But because moral law exceeds humanity itself, these universal laws need the law to come from a higher power. The argument proclaims this to be God.

The moral argument is unavoidable and it forms the standards of all our behaviours and thoughts. For instance, why do you live the way you do? Why do you follow even the simplest of laws? Like stopping at red lights or waiting to pay for groceries, etc. Everything we do is all upheld within the very fabric of our social programming from the likes of parents, siblings, family, peers, and friends.

As a child, I was taught that if someone hits you, then you hit them back twice as hard. Although this wasn't something that I challenged, and as my brother and I got older, we would fight, sad to say, a lot. I remember on one occasion when I tried to stab my brother with a knife in frustration and anger. When abnormal becomes normal, because you know no other way, you are numb to the implications.

On 7 November 2007, Pekka-Eric Auvinen killed nine people and injured dozens of others in his school in Finland. Auvinen declared his evolutionary beliefs being that 'human life is not sacred… Death is not a tragedy; it happens in nature all the time between all species. Not all human lives are important or worth saving'.[11]

If our morality is not grounded in God, then it becomes hopelessly subjective, because to reject moral values as meaningless is logically impossible. If morality is something that we have merely invented, then our moral behaviour has no ultimate meaning, significance, or importance.[12]

In a world without God, there is no apparent difference between good and evil. Otherwise, there is no way to prove that murder is wrong.

However, I believe there is a Creator, and He has a law that says:

'*You must not murder*'. Exodus 20:13

The Biological Argument

The Greek word *bios* means 'life'; and basically, science has tried to prove that life can come from matter alone, and not just from pre-existent life. On the other hand is the creationist view of believing that the universe and life itself originated by divine creation.

At some point, I believe, when you trace all forms of life back to a source, you will ultimately find God, because He is the life source (John 14:6) and possesses eternal life Himself. (Psalm 90:2).

So, I guess the ultimate question concerning this argument is whether life occurred naturally or as a result of our Creator?

The Bible says that Jesus gives us eternal life, which means that we will never perish. But this is concerning our spirit and not the physical body. 2 Corinthians confirms this:

'*That is why we never give up. Though our bodies are dying, our spirits are being renewed every day*'. 2 Corinthians 4:16

So, what is my point?

Science has tried to conduct experiments to indicate that spontaneous life can occur. However, theories time after time have been proven incorrect once science has advanced.

We now know that life does not occur spontaneously, anywhere, or at any time in the past. Additionally, the mathematical approaches used by scientists to formulate the likelihood of life forming on earth by naturalistic means has been concluded a basic impossibility.[13]

It is unfortunate that there are so many people in the world, even in my own life, who hold on to the argument that life comes from nothing. Things that I learned within my science classes at school formed incorrect viewpoints in my own life, decades after being taught them. And although God has revealed His truths to me now, for others, it has possibly shaped generations of people who live under the pretence that science proves against God. Discoveries have changed everything in science, even since I have been alive on this earth.

The information that we learn can lead us to God, but we can only receive Him by faith, and faith alone. Therefore, it's more about humbling ourselves, because certain things have been hidden from our hearts:

> *'At that time Jesus prayed this prayer: "O Father, Lord of heaven and earth, thank you for hiding these things from those who think themselves wise and clever, and for revealing them to the childlike"'.* Matthew 11:25

Jesus mentions two kinds of people in His prayer: the 'wise' who are arrogant in their knowledge; and the 'childlike' who are open to receiving the truth of God's Word. As mentioned previously, only God holds all of the answers, and science never contradicts the Word of God. It's merely that we do not know all of the fundamental information, yet.

Therefore, from information that we can determine from, it only leaves the supernatural option as viable; and this is the creationists' viewpoint, which has never changed.

Life had to be created. It could not have happened naturally.

The Historical Argument

When people ask about the historical evidence for Jesus, they generally ask the question with wanting the answer to come from outside of the Bible.

I find it amazing that some people do not think of the Bible as credible evidence for God's existence. The Bible is teeming with references to Christ within the synoptic Gospels—Matthew, Mark, and Luke—and within the Pauline letters written by the apostle Paul. New Testament scholars have enormous amounts of the ancient manuscript as evidence to prove not only His existence but also His divinity.

Historians believe that the Gospel of Mark was the first Gospel written around AD 70. Not everyone agrees with this and there are those who date the writing of the Gospels in the second century; more than one hundred years after Jesus died.

However, even if this were true, regarding ancient historical evidence, writings less than two hundred years after the event took place are considered very reliable.[14] When people begin movements, it is not until many generations later that people record things about them.

The fact is we have better historical documentation for Jesus than for the founder of any other ancient religion. Even without the Bible, historical figures such as Josephus, the Talmud, Tacitus, and Pliny the Younger, who are ancient non-Christian sources, provide us with historical evidence; and therefore, we would still be able to draw the same conclusion about Jesus.[15]

Historian Michael Grant wrote: 'If we apply to the New Testament the same sort of criteria as we should apply to other ancient writings containing historical material, we can no more reject Jesus' existence…then we can reject those whose reality as historical figures is never questioned'.[16] In other words, to reject Christ's existence and divinity because of the amount of evidence we have compared to other people would mean that you have to dismiss all of our histories. Now there is a sobering thought!

The first reason as to why the historical argument for Christ is so strong is because of the number of early copies of ancient manuscripts that have been found, which is astounding.

These are the number of copies made off the originals and were obviously before the printing press. We have tens of thousands of copies of the manuscripts, plus thousands of quotes from the early Church fathers.

Secondly, historians have dated the time span—the time between the original and the earliest copies being made—at around thirty years after Christ's death.

Why does this matter either way? Especially, if you don't believe in the existence of Christ. It matters because the world's history is made up of the copies that have survived from primary and secondary sources using historical methods, to write events. This is called textual criticism.

So compare the New Testament copies that people want to disregard to the likes of Julius Caesar. Historians have found copies to be written 1,000 years after initially being written and that only ten copies have been found! But, we still believe that Caesar is credible within historical accounts.

Only seven copies of Greek philosopher Plato's works have ever been found and they have been discovered to be dated 1,200 years after the originals were written.

Tacitus, who wrote about Jesus, was a Roman historian and senator. He wrote the *Annals,* and are believed to be an essential source for our understanding into the history of the Roman Empire during the first century. However, only three copies have survived and the time span was 900 years after Tacitus first wrote them.[17]

One of the most significant pieces of evidence for the existence of Jesus Christ and the historical argument of Jesus being whom He claimed to be, is that thousands of Christians, including the apostles, were willing to give their lives as martyrs. All of which was documented and history shows us that 2,000 years after Christ's death, people are continuing to die for their belief in Him.

The Christological Argument

The Christological argument has to be one of the most significant cases for Jesus. Only because let's be honest, if Christ didn't come from a virgin birth, have a sinless life, perform miracles, teach God's love, die on the cross, and if He wasn't buried and resurrected on the third day and then ascended to Heaven, then Christianity is flawed and life for us has no purpose.

So then my question would be, what is the point of it all?

This argument looks at things from the wisdom of Jesus, His deity, and the resurrection. All of Jesus' life is unexplainable, apart from Him being God, the Messiah, as He claimed to be. Jesus Christ is the greatest revelation of God's existence.

All He was, all He did, and all He said attests to the existence of God.[18] Everything that I am, personally, comes from the redeeming work of humanity through Christ. John 1:14-18 even testifies to this, but I love that Jesus brought truth to His claims and Paul bluntly puts this in the following Scripture:

> *'And if Christ has not been raised, our preaching is useless and so is your faith'.* 1 Corinthians 15:14 NIV

Reflect on these points:[19]
- Jesus' claims are consistent with His life.

- Jesus' claims are consistent with the entire revelation of God, general and special revelation.
- Jesus' claims are consistent with the reality in which we live in.
- Jesus' claims are consistent with our faith experiences.
- Jesus' claims are consistent with His resurrection.

If we reject the claims that Christ made, then how do we account for His resurrection?

Luke was a historian and physician. He wrote the books of Luke and Acts in the Bible, and he was the only Gentile to write any part of the New Testament. (Colossians 4:11-14) Luke was well educated, observant, and a careful writer; therefore his books are teeming with historical and geographical facts.

Sir William Mitchell Ramsay (1851-1939) was an archaeologist and Bible sceptic. He declared that the book of Acts was full of errors; and therefore to prove this contention, he travelled to Asia Minor to demonstrate Luke's unreliability.

Sir Ramsay understood that he could not prove or disprove miracle accounts, but if he could show Luke to be a sloppy historian on facts that could be verified, he felt he could then discredit Luke's unverifiable stories because the other accounts were merely messy reports.[20]

Ramsay's study led him to conclude that 'Luke's history is unsurpassed in respect to its trustworthiness' and 'Luke is a historian of the first rank; not merely are his statements trustworthy...this author should be placed along with the very greatest of historians'.[21]

Therefore, taking into account that Luke is deemed to be one of the greatest historians and factually correct, Luke writes:

'To whom He also presented Himself alive after His suffering by many infallible proofs, being seen by them during forty days and speaking of the things pertaining to the kingdom of God'. Acts 1:3 NKJV

We cannot credit Luke for being truthful in only part of his work. The resurrection demonstrates Christ's deity because it becomes the foundation of our faith.

'For no one can lay any foundation other than the one already laid, which is Jesus Christ'. 1 Corinthians 3:11 NIV

The Bibliological Argument

Bibliology is the study of the Bible, the Word of God. The Bible is therefore, inspired knowledge about God. The Bible not only reveals who God is, to us, but also His purpose for our lives.

This argument shows us that God inspires the Bible, and studying the Bible has taught us God's attributes. About who He is and what God is like. A lot of unbelievers like to use the Bible itself as an argument because they feel the Bible is flawed; that it has errors or contradictions because human authors wrote it.

The Bible, after all, is a collection of sixty-six books written by about forty different people, over some sixteen hundred years. Also, these people were from different cultures and countries, and they had different roles to play in society. For instance, some were kings, prophets, others were fishermen and even prisoners, but the fact remains that the Bible was written in three languages and most of the people who wrote the different books never actually met each other but they produced an amazingly unified book that as a whole never contradicts itself.

Bruce M. Metzger who was a world-class scholar at Princeton Theological Seminary and expert in ancient biblical manuscripts said that 'the modern New Testament is 99.5 percent free of textual discrepancies, with no major Christian doctrines in doubt',[22] which seems to make the Bible pretty infallible, in my opinion!

God gave the authors *revelation* of truth, which could not be discovered by their natural reasoning. All that God reveals about Himself is found within Scripture where God has ultimately shown His true nature, character, and being, which are His attributes, as mentioned previously.

God *inspired* these people to write down what was revealed to them in their own unique and personal way, which surely makes the Bible more credible as there are slight differences with the Gospels. If they were all identical, then people would say that the writers conspired about what they were going to say in advance, casting doubt of being independent of each other.

Lastly, God gave the writers *illumination* to enlighten their understanding to receive the revelation given by God. So in short, revelation is the reception of truth.

Inspiration is the recording of truth and illumination is the perception of truth, brought about from the Holy Spirit.[23] Illumination is again, *rhema*, which we talked about in the last chapter.

I love the Scripture in Jeremiah, where it says:

> *'If you look for me wholeheartedly, you will find me'.* Jeremiah 29:13

You can find the revelation of Jesus within every book of the Bible.[24] That's how much God wants to reveal Himself to us.

Another reason we know that God inspired the Bible is by prophecy and fulfilment, because prophecy is seen as evidence of divine knowledge.

The Messianic Prophecy was possibly the greatest example of this. Did you know that before Jesus was even born that thirty different people foretold the Lord Jesus Christ over a period of 4,000 years? And they prophesied when these events occurred; approximately 330 Old Testament prophecies were fulfilled.

Mathematicians have put the possibility of this happening to anyone like this:[25]
- One person fulfilling eight prophecies: 1 in 100,000,000,000,000,000.
- One person able to fulfil forty-eight prophecies: 1 chance in 10 to the 157th power.
- One person who fulfilled 300+ prophecies: Only Jesus!

In all honesty, no human will ever be able to comprehend these things because it they are God-sized; but through God's Word, we can wholeheartedly continue to seek after Him[26] so that He will continue to reveal Himself more to us.

The Bible has been the most loved and yet the most hated book in human existence.

The Guinness World Records has recently estimated that more than five billion copies of the Bible have been printed. People have given orders for the Bible to be destroyed. Bibles have been burned, and Christian's have died for even possessing it. Others continue to reject, corrupt, and challenge it, from every angle; and yet through all the centuries, the Bible has survived to remain the most significant book in history. It continues to be the world's number one best-selling, nonfiction book—yet Bible sales are now no longer counted in weekly figures.

With regards to the canon of Scripture being reliable, it's again one of the topics that people like to cling to and try and pull apart. They believe that since man put the Bible together that we can't be sure that God inspired the Bible we read today.

Some people do not like that the Church voted on discounting any book that was contradictory. Yes, there are books that contradicted others and so were left out, but the reason why they were left out is simple. The Jewish Scriptures, called Tanakh, and the Christian Old Testament are identical, but they have a different order. Concerning the New Testament, the writings had to be either from eyewitnesses, in this case Matthew and John—or first-generation

Christians who knew the eyewitnesses within the first century, such as the apostles or pastors of the early Church.

Therefore, any book that didn't make it into the Bible should be seen as exciting reads but they are unsound documents and not the inspired Word of God. Also, those people did not meet the criteria mentioned, along with other principles, which the councils followed.

Ultimately, it was God who decided what books belonged in the biblical canon. Scripture, which exists in the canon today, are the books where God inspired their writing. It was merely a matter of God convincing people which books should be included in the canon.

There is no denying that billions of lives have been changed by its truth, including my own; and therefore, these things show more proof of Scripture being inspired by God.

Bibliology teaches us that the Bible is from God and therefore all Scripture is useful to us, for preparing us to walk through all the different seasons in our lives. (2 Timothy 3:16-17)

> **'Many have quarrelled about religion that never practiced it'.**
> **Benjamin Franklin**

Has It Become Obvious Yet?

Simply put. Life as a Christian is all about faith: having faith in God and believing that Jesus Christ is the Lord and Saviour of our lives.

As I mentioned at the start of the chapter, I wrote about these arguments not to convince you, but to encourage you. As a

Christian, we influence the sphere that God has given to us, and therefore, sometimes, our faith is humbly stepping out of our comfort zone to provide an answer as to why we believe what we do! Other times, it recognises that we're not meant to have all the answers, but to trust in the One who does. These arguments merely show what God has spoken about all along, and I hope they have you thinking!

But I want to encourage you that the reason that God chose faith as the way that we become right with Him is that He wanted to base the whole thing on His beautiful grace, because then our boasting is eliminated and His glory is exalted. Our pride is then put down when God's splendour is lifted up, and our salvation is made sure,[27] when we choose to walk in the purpose that God predestined for us, before time even began.

For the rest of this book, I go through the strongholds that we can carry and look at what the Word of God says about them, in order to break free.

Life's Greatest Battles is becoming aware of what lies the enemy uses against us so we do not find freedom in our lives. But God does want freedom for us because we were created for a purpose, and with purpose, to have a relationship with Him.

CHAPTER FOUR

SUFFERING WITH A LOVING GOD

How Can God Love Us When There Is so Much Pain in the World?

> *'Out of suffering have emerged the strongest souls'.*
> **Kahlil Gibran**

His Thoughts Versus Ours

Would you call God loving when there is not one person who can escape or ignore the suffering within this world? Unfortunately Christians cannot give a straightforward answer with regards to this subject. But I know from experience. I would look at someone and try to mumble my way through an explanation as to why a loved one had developed cancer, or why a child suffered in a cruel and unthinkable way.

Most times, I would be pleading with God, in my head, to take me to Heaven at that point, so I didn't have to feel uncomfortable, because this topic has to be a huge stumbling block for most people, in being able to believe that God is love. (1 John 4:8)

Therefore, I hope to address some of those concerns people have. No, I am not God; but if I can help people to break down the barriers we may have against God Himself, then I feel it is worth exploring this issue.

C.S. Lewis was from Northern Ireland and an unbeliever; but once he found Christ, he reflected, 'My argument against God was that the universe seemed so cruel and unjust. But how had I got this idea of just and unjust? A man does not call a line crooked unless he has some idea of a straight line'.[28]

So what is my point?

People stand on their moral principles and charge God for breaking them; but where did the principle come from in the first place?

Looking back at my days as a nonbeliever, I had so much hatred and resentment towards God because of the evil and suffering that exists in the world. Yet my belief system was to believe there was no God, so there shouldn't have been anyone to be resentful against in the first place!

Suffering in this Messed Up World

Suffering is still one of the most frequently raised objections to the Christian faith, so I don't think we can overlook it.

We see suffering on a global scale such as World Wars, within a community such as the attack on the World Trade Centre, and lastly on an individual level with grief, sickness, persecution, etc.

So, I want to ask some questions for us to ponder: Where is a loving God in a messed-up world? And why would a good and loving God allow such tragedies to happen?

Firstly, remember that His ways are not our ways and His thoughts not our thoughts, because He is God, and we are not! (Isaiah 55:9)

Paul reiterates this in the book of Romans:

> *'Oh, how great are God's riches, and wisdom, and knowledge! How impossible it is for us to understand his decisions and his ways! For who can know the Lord's thoughts? Who knows enough to give him advice'?* Romans 11:33-34

Secondly, we need to know that God is not responsible for the acts we do, regardless of whether He could stop the things from occurring or not.

God created us with the potential or the capacity to choose between good and evil or right from wrong. In other words, the possibility of evil God created, but not its reality.

Sin is simply the abuse of your free will.

How easy is it for us to blame others?

Suffering Through the Generations

The Bible shows us that we have done this since humanity was first created. Adam blamed Eve, and then Eve blamed the serpent.

To give you some context of the serpent, he was renamed satan after originally being called *lucifer* (Latin) or *helel* (Hebrew) which both mean 'Morning Star'. He was not content with his position of guardian angel in Heaven; and because of his beauty, his heart was proud and his wisdom corrupted (Ezekiel 28:17), so he desired to be higher than God, and *that was actually the beginning of sin* (Isaiah 14:12-15).

Interestingly enough, satan used the very same temptation in the Garden of Eden when Adam and Eve rebelled against the will of God; he said to Eve:

'You shall be as God'. Genesis 3:5

Unfortunately, this means that since then, sin has been passed down through all of the generations of humankind because we are Adam's descendants. Therefore, we inherit his nature, which is intrinsically wrong; and whether we like to admit it or not, we all go against God.

'The wages of sin is death…', Romans 6:23

The Scripture in Romans shows just how bad we are compared to what God intended for us; and yet God still loves us more than we could ever comprehend. That is why God has given us a gift that's unmerited or undeserved, which is mentioned in the second part of that Scripture in Romans 6:

'…but the free gift of God is eternal life through Christ Jesus our Lord'. Romans 6:23

The Choice to Love

So why did God put humans on earth, knowing that Adam and Eve would sin and therefore bring evil, death, and suffering on all humanity? And why didn't He create us all and leave us in Heaven where we would be perfect and without pain?

Suffering was not part of God's original created order. (Genesis 1-2.) There was no suffering in the world before humanity rebelled, only the ability for satan to tempt us. Although, there will be no more suffering when God creates a new Heaven and a new earth. (Revelation 21)

The truth is, God chose to do this because He loves us and wanted to give us *free will*. Love is not love if it is forced, and it can only be love if there is a real choice.

God gave human beings a choice and the freedom to love or not to love.

Being given this freedom, men and women from the beginning have still chosen to break God's laws. The result is, unfortunately, suffering.

There are different ways that we can suffer, and I would like to talk about some of these ways briefly. Although, this chapter in some ways will only touch the surface of this challenging subject.

Our Sin

Some suffering we endure is the result of our sin. Tough to hear, I know, but God made the world built on moral foundations, and there is a natural connection between sin and consequences.

For instance, if a person abuses drugs, drug addiction may be the consequence. If people drink excessively, they may eventually suffer from alcoholism. Similarly, selfishness, greed, lust, arrogance, and bad temper often lead to broken relationships and unhappiness of one sort or another.[29]

In a later chapter, I will talk more about my 'bad' relationships. However, I remember thinking as a new Christian that I was a 'good person' and I did not have any of those character traits in my life, so why was I classed as a sinner? I was not greedy or bad-tempered, but I now understand that I had a limited understanding of how the devil works in this world. I was looking at those character traits as being things that people would see as evident in my life. I now know that God judges a person's thoughts as well as his or her actions, because Jesus proclaimed that our efforts are the result of what is ultimately in our hearts (Matthew 12:34).

Please understand that the enemy uses our thoughts to tempt us—that is not a sin as we cannot control what comes into our mind; but when we take action on them, it causes us to stumble:

> '...take every thought captive to obey Christ'.
> 2 Corinthians 10:5 ESV

> **'Although the world is full of suffering,**
> **it is also full of the overcoming of it'.**
> *Helen Keller*

Suffering Does Not Mean We Have Sinned

On the other hand, we do need to recognise that *not all* suffering is the result of our sin. Job was blameless in God's eyes, yet he still suffered immensely.

Job's friends thought that Job's suffering was because of the sin in his life, but they were wrong, and God confirmed this in Job 42:7-8. One of the most beautiful pictures to me was Job refusing to curse God for his suffering when talking to his wife:

> *'..."You talk like a foolish woman. Should we accept only good things from the hand of God and never anything bad?" So in all this, Job said nothing wrong'.* Job 2:10

How easy is it to accept the good but not want the tough times in life?

Jesus also confirms that suffering is not the direct result of our sins, in John 9:1-3 where the disciples asked Jesus who had sinned, the blind man or his parents? The blind man had been blind since birth:

> *'"Neither this man nor his parents sinned," said Jesus, "but this happened so that the works of God might be displayed in him"'.* John 9:3 NIV

We, therefore, should not automatically think if people or ourselves are suffering, then something has been done wrong.

As mentioned before, it is crucial for us to examine our hearts because our actions are the fruit of our thoughts. We should be cautious about making judgments about others and ourselves because this can cause guilt and shame in lives by thinking suffering is punishment.

This is not the message of the gospel.

How do we, therefore, distinguish between punishment and discipline?

Remember, as a Christian, our sin: whether past, present, or future; has already been abolished on the cross through Jesus. *As Christians, we will never be punished for sin.* That was done once for all. (Romans 8:1)

Discipline Is Different From Suffering

However, if we sin as Christians, the sin that remains in our lives does sometimes require God's discipline. If we continue to act in ways that do not represent God well, and also do not repent and turn from that sin, God brings His divine discipline upon us. If God did not, He would not be a loving Father.

Just as I need to discipline and guide my daughter, our heavenly Father also lovingly corrects us, for our benefit.

Hebrews 12:7-11 tells us: *'As you endure this divine discipline, remember that God is treating you as his own children. Who ever heard of a child who is never disciplined by its father? If God doesn't discipline you as he does all of his children, it means that you are illegitimate and are not really his children at all. Since we respected our earthly fathers who disciplined us, shouldn't we submit even more to the discipline of the Father of our spirits, and live forever? For our earthly fathers disciplined us for a few years, doing the best they knew how. But God's discipline is always good for us, so that we might share in his holiness. No discipline is enjoyable while it is happening—it's painful! But afterward there will be a peaceful harvest of right living for those who are trained in this way.'*

Discipline then is how God lovingly turns His children, us, from rebellion to obedient, because through discipline, our eyes are opened more clearly to God's perspective in our lives. In Psalm 32, David tells us that discipline causes us to confess and repent of sins that we have not yet dealt with in life.

I remember as a child being called into our house and being confronted by my mum. She would be expecting my brother or me to confess to whatever she had found out, only for her to be met with myself as a blubbering mess because of spilling my heart out to all the wrongs my brother had done that I could think of in that split second!

In this way discipline is cleansing. It is also where we grow spiritually. The more we know about God, the more we get to know about His desires for our lives.

We need to consider that sin is constantly seeking to take root in our lives while on earth. Therefore, we not only have to deal with God's discipline for our disobedience, but we also have to deal with the worldly consequences of sin:

Romans 3:10 says: *'No one is righteous—not even one'*.

God Forgives

When we do something that goes against God, God will forgive us if we ask for forgiveness and cleanse us from that sin, which then restores our relationship with Him.

However, the worldly consequences of sin must be endured. For instance, if you murder someone, the result would be to go to prison.

I love that God works even through those consequences to increase our faith and glorify Himself. C.S. Lewis points out, 'God whispers to us in our pleasures, speaks in our conscience, but shouts in our pains: it is His megaphone to rouse a deaf world'.[30]

I had heard so many stories over the years of where a person had met Christ when they thought they had nothing more to offer this world. It's as if when the world spits us out in its corruptness, we finally hear God's voice.

We then understand that the stillness within the chaos is an oxymoron in which we have found our lives. It makes no sense and yet it still brings us to our knees; because it is the very place that we should have been all along: seeking God.

If we are suffering, then there are a few questions we can ask ourselves, which are:[31]

Is this suffering a result of my sin?

If it is, we can ask God to reveal the specific sin. What am I that goes against God? God will never leave us with the feeling of guilt. That kind of condemnation may come from satan, but never from

God. If there is something that we need to ask for forgiveness from, then seek God and turn away from it, for good.

What are You saying to me through this?

There may be some particular lesson that God wants to teach us.

What do You want me to do?

We need to hold on to our hope found in Jesus. This life is always a mixture of battle and blessing. In times of conflict, we need to remember that they do not last forever, and often a blessing is just around the corner.

When the Innocent Suffer Through Others

We have so far looked at the sin in our lives and briefly why we have a choice to love God, no matter what we are going through. But for this next section, I want to concentrate on when we suffer through others' actions.

Much of what Jesus taught, was through parables (stories). One of His most well-known parables is the Lost Son (Luke 15:11-32) a story of love, rejection, suffering, and forgiveness.

It's a story of a father and his two sons. It unfolds with the younger son seeking his inheritance before his father died. In other words, he could not wait for his father to die, he wanted his portion of wealth now!

The selfishness of the younger son leads him to disaster because he took what was going to be allocated to him before the correct time. When we force things, our flesh is in action; and when that happens, destruction is not far away. In leaving his father's house, his father's protection, and everything he needed for that time of his life, he took a journey that took him to eat what was considered unclean as an Israelite—swine food! In the depths of the suffering that he inflicts on himself through free will (God did not do this), he comes to his senses and decides to return home. To the younger son's surprise, he finds his father waiting for him.

Bear in mind that in the period to which Jesus told this story, a nobleman would never run in public, and yet the father rushes towards his lost son and hugs and kisses him with his heart bursting with compassion.

Then despite the jealous concern of the older brother, the father throws a party to celebrate the lost son's return.

One point that Jesus was making was that in spite of the son's foolishness, the father never gave up on him. In fact, the father suffered intensely at the thought of his lost son.

The father in this parable is God, so it is important to note that no matter how much we go against God or how much suffering we endure, God will never abandon us.

The suffering we face only causes God to run further into this world and onto a cross. God endured suffering to the end, through Jesus Christ, and this shows His solidarity with a world in which every person suffers.[32]

This entire situation still begs the question: 'Why'? Why, if God is loving and just, does He not step in and do something about the state of the world and rid us of everything that causes us, His children, to suffer?

My answer to this is free will.

We want God to step into situations that are bad, yet for some of God's children, we neglect our relationship with Him when it suits us. To be a disciple, as already mentioned, is to follow the teacher, His ways, at all times.

God gave us the free will to choose (Joshua 24:14-15) whether to love Him and others. We have the freedom to bless each other and help someone in their time of need. To choose to believe in what the Word of God says over the world's opinion.

Friend, we have the free will to choose to help make this world as God intended it to be. We have been given all the tools to live in perfect peace, without fear or hatred. So why do we need God to step in when things are tough? He is always with us. He will always guide and protect us. God makes a way when there isn't one; and so for us to witness to others, we need to show them who God is in our lives!

So for me, I have gone through hardships; more than some people, and less than others. Does this make me an expert? No, but I feel that God stepping in for everything that is occurring in the world goes against our free will.

Remember, we all can choose regarding our actions.

The Bible speaks about us being strengthened, and I have seen that a tragedy can give me an overwhelming dependence on God. We may assume that we are blessed when life goes well or cursed when it doesn't, but trouble can be a blessing when it makes us stronger, and prosperity is a curse if it takes us away from God; but either way, we need God. After all, I believe Jesus was highly blessed from the point of being born in a stable to being raised from the dead. But who would call the cross blessed? Yet without the cross, we would not have life.

In the book *Extreme Devotion: The Voice of the Martyrs*, a Chinese Christian experienced persecution and had the following to say, 'Where there is no cross, there is no crown…If the spices are not refined to become oil, the fragrance of the perfume cannot flow forth; and if the grapes are not crushed in the vat, they will not become wine'.[33]

Is Anyone Pure in This World?

Can I pose another question?

Is there anyone who is innocent and pure? Harsh, I know.

I immediately think of a child. As far as humanity would deem, a child should never suffer, and should never know pain or hardship, but yet the Bible says:

> 'For all have sinned and fall short of the glory of God'.
> Romans 3:23 NKJV

You read earlier that we all have inherited Adam's sinful nature; nonetheless with all of us, as I mentioned, we have the freedom of choice.

Although with that comes the inevitable; that it is just a matter of time before we go against each other and God, as it's not something we are taught: *it is who we are.*

The first time my little girl, Sarai, told a lie, she was around two years old and I felt that I had been punched in the stomach. I felt like a bad parent, but I had never taught her to lie. I realised that it unfortunately just comes naturally within us.

Parents don't generally let their children disobey them, and this is not because the parents are egomaniacs, it's because they love their children.

For instance, even if my daughter doesn't grasp why Kieren, my husband, and I have rules that are for her own good, there are going to be circumstances when she cannot understand all of the details. She simply just needs to know that Mum and Dad said no.

The same thing applies to God. There's nothing unreasonable about God's expectation of obedience, given that He is a loving Father who wants the best for His children. And let's be honest, God knows far more than we do!

When Would We Want It All to Stop?

To play devil's advocate, how much suffering would we want God to stop? Is it fairer that an older person dies than a younger one? Isn't death, no matter at what age, distressing for the person's family and friends?

Let me put it another way. If it was 'unfair' for all the school children to die from a mass shooting in the United States, then for

God to be 'fair', shouldn't He prevent all deaths of all school-aged children, in every tragedy, everywhere?

If God did do that, we would then conclude that He should also prevent children from dying of cancer or starvation.

So let's assume that God chose to stop all deaths in children, anywhere, anytime. But if He decided to define childhood as ending at 18 years old, why would it be fair to allow a 19 year old to die, while preventing all death under that age?

This abstract questioning shows that, logically, we could not be satisfied with any of the world's suffering or fairness of who lives or dies within those circumstances, until death has been eliminated.[34]

My dad has said that if God loved me, then He wouldn't let me or any other Christian suffer. But if every time we encountered difficulties we were able to make them vanish like the morning dew disappearing from the heat of the sun, then it is likely that we would never mature enough to become more like Christ, which is God's ultimate desire for us.

The author of Hebrews writes to show us what happened when Jesus suffered:

> 'Even though Jesus was God's Son, he learned obedience from the things he suffered'. Hebrews 5:8

Then Paul tells us what can happen if we do the same:

'We can rejoice, too, when we run into problems and trials, for we know that they help us develop endurance. And endurance develops strength of character, and character strengthens our confident hope of salvation. And this hope will not lead to disappointment. For we know how dearly God loves us, because he has given us the Holy Spirit to fill our hearts with his love'. Romans 5:3-5

God Is the Supplier of All Our Needs

I feel an essential point to bear in mind is that God still sustains us and will supply all our needs, despite the original act of creating humanity in the first place.

Some people might like to think of the world as more like a watch, which becomes independent of its creator once made. They then see Jesus as the 'repair guy', because the watch is broken. But the truth is, God never left His creation.

Like the potter with clay, He is making everything new (Revelation 21:5), God is working in and through His creation. We are not finished until Jesus returns. Until that day, God knows there are flaws in the world, weaknesses, and imperfections; so He will continue to mould us; shaping us as seems best to Him (Jeremiah 18:4), which is that we grow into who we were ultimately created to be.

Our world is a place where evil, injustice, and suffering prevail. Blaming individuals or God does not alleviate the hurt that is felt. But there is hope for the future, as God is not only the Judge but also our Saviour. He is the God of justice and mercy.

One day God will act upon all of the cruel and defiant people in the world, and He will also have mercy on those who come under His authority. God's timing is always perfect, but God is delaying His judgment, which I feel is a good thing, so that more people can find Him, as they accept Jesus into their hearts.

Imagine if God did get rid of all the evil today and how many millions of lost souls there would be, compared to His waiting and allowing those souls a little more time to seek and accept Him:

> *'The Lord isn't really being slow about his promise, as some people think. No, he is being patient for your sake. He does not want anyone to be destroyed, but wants everyone to repent'.* 2 Peter 3:9

That is the reason He is waiting so long to give judgment over the world; He wants us all to think again about our lives and to open ourselves up to Him.

We are free to choose Christ, to ignore Him, or even resist Him because as I keep reminding, God has given us the free will to do so.

However, opening ourselves up to Christ will not safeguard us against the pain and suffering this world offers, but it will ensure that God will be there through every situation in our lives. He will be transforming us through the pain so that we will be the light for others to see Him working in us, and during those trying times, He will lead us beside quiet waters to refresh our soul, so that we might find rest.

The Long Silence by John Stott

This playlet, *The Long Silence*, was written many years ago and therefore some of the language is not commonly used today but it powerfully reminds us that Christ suffered more than we can ever comprehend and therefore He can empathise with us because of the pain He endured on the cross:

At the end of time, billions of people were seated on a great plain before God's throne. Most shrank back from the brilliant light before them. But some groups near the front talked heatedly, not cringing with cringing shame – but with belligerence. "Can God judge us? How can He know about suffering?", snapped a pert young brunette. She ripped open a sleeve to reveal a tattooed number from a Nazi concentration camp. "We endured terror…beatings…torture…death!" In another group, a boy lowered his collar. "What about this?" he demanded, showing an ugly rope burn. "Lynched, for no crime but being black!" In another crowd there was a pregnant schoolgirl with sullen eyes: "Why should I suffer?" she murmured. "It wasn't my fault." Far out across the plain were hundreds of such groups. Each had a complaint against God for the evil and suffering He had permitted in His world. How lucky God was to live in Heaven, where all was sweetness and light. Where there was no weeping or fear, no hunger or hatred. What did God know of all that man had been forced to endure in this world? For God leads a pretty sheltered life, they said. So each of these groups sent forth their leader, chosen because he had suffered the most.

A Jew, a black person from Hiroshima, a horribly deformed arthritic, a thalidomide child. In the centre of the vast plain, they consulted with each other. At last, they were ready to present their case. It was rather clever. Before God could be qualified to be their judge, He must endure what they had endured. Their decision was that God should be sentenced to live on earth as a man. Let him be born a Jew. Let the legitimacy of his birth be doubted. Give him a work so difficult that even his family will think him out of his mind. Let him be betrayed by his closest friends. Let him face false charges, be tried by a prejudiced jury and convicted by a cowardly judge. Let him be tortured. At the last, let him see what it means to be terribly alone. Then let him die so there can be no doubt he died. Let there be a great host of witnesses to verify it.

As each leader announced his portion of the sentence, loud murmurs of approval went up from the throng of people assembled. When the last had finished pronouncing sentence, there was a long silence. No one uttered a word. No one moved. For suddenly, all knew that God had already served His sentence.[35]

'Suffering is actually at the heart of the Christian story'.
Timothy Keller

How Do We Respond to Suffering?

At some point, we need realise that we will face disappointment and pain in some aspects of our lives. But it is how we continue to trust God, give Him thanks, and choose to rejoice in Him that will bring a blessing in our lives that the world cannot comprehend.

My daughter was around 14 months old when she was taken to hospital by ambulance. The paediatrician told us that an infection caused by teething had spread to her brain. They were unsure if they had treated it in time.

Sarai lay in the bed motionless and my reaction at first was to become angry with God. Numerous doctors had told me that I would never have children, and so I stood sobbing, watching helplessly as our miracle child fought for her life.

How *dare* God try and take her away from me! She was mine!

I initially demanded that God save her. The demands then became more of a plea. A plea that God would take away this bug, in Jesus' name. And then the pleas became nothing more than an uncontrollable swell of emotion that overtook my body. As I softly placed my head on my child's lap, I could not move. Paralysed with fear, I cried for what seemed like an eternity.

Sometimes it seems impossible to obey the commands God gives us in His Word. However, as God enables us to understand the good that can come through anguish, (Romans 8:28) we will know that it is possible to obey those 'impossible' directions because we see life from a new perspective.

That day was the first time I heard the audible voice of God, and He quietly said to me, 'She is mine'. It changed my perspective, and it changed my life forever. I realised that what we hold on to in this world the enemy uses against us. God is the Creator, and we are the created.

Do We Trust God When Faced with Difficulty?

In that split second, I remembered Abraham's willingness to sacrifice his son, Isaac. Then the peace of God fell upon me; in my soul, I knew that if all I had was fourteen beautiful months of knowing what it was to be a mother, then I was blessed abundantly for that time.

So my reply was only this, 'Your will be done'. I did not think that God wanted my daughter to die, that is not the God we have read about in this chapter. But God is all-knowing, and therefore He knows more than we ever could. Therefore, we need to trust that the outcome, no matter what it is, serves a more significant purpose than we may ever know or understand in this lifetime.

As mentioned, if Jesus learned obedience by the things that He suffered, then so can we, because it shows us Scriptures like:

'If we endure hardship, we will reign with him'. 2 Timothy 2:12

And,

'God called you to do good, even if it means suffering, just as Christ suffered for you...'. 1 Peter 2:21

When we obey God's Word, especially when it does not make sense, we learn through experience that God's ways indeed are the best. In the end, we find that His will is exactly what we would have chosen if we had identified all the facts.

I know people who have lost children, and I cannot imagine the pain felt from this, but all of them are still walking closely with Christ and being obedient to the call on their lives because of the love they have for God.

None of us have perfect lives, and we need to know that we will not be free from suffering. Having this perspective can bring more of a healthy balance to our lives because we do not miss out on the things we can experience in this lifetime through Christ, and we are also expectant with what is to come when He returns.

My daughter was healed and Kieren, my husband, eventually came to Christ through that painful journey. But the reason I shared this story with you was to merely show you that God is good all the time, even in the midst of our pain. Only God can turn a mess into a message.

Helping Others Through the Pain

The parable of the Good Samaritan (Luke 10:25-37) makes clear that we are not to pass others by who are suffering. We should always stop and have compassion for people, by making ourselves available in any way possible to help them.

Jesus commanded us to:

'Love your neighbour as yourself'. Mark 12:31

We cannot always keep this law because of our human nature; our heart and desires are mostly selfish. Therefore, this shows us that we all need Jesus as much as each other!

The parable found in Luke's Gospel teaches us that when helping others through pain:
- We are to set aside our prejudice and show love and compassion for others.
- Our neighbour is anyone we encounter; we are all God's children, and we are to love all of humanity as Jesus has taught.
- Keeping the law in its entirety with the intent to save ourselves is an impossible task; we need the Saviour, Jesus. Showing the love of Christ will hopefully allow us to share the Gospel with others.

We can do all of this because of our relationship with God:

'...God is our merciful Father and the source of all comfort. He comforts us in all our troubles so that we can comfort others...'. 2 Corinthians 1:3-4

Jesus, our example, showed us to fight against suffering whenever we come across it. Jesus in His ministry fed the hungry, healed the sick, and raised the dead. (Matthew 10:8) Jesus brought Good News to the poor, proclaimed captives will be released, the blind will see, and the oppressed will be set free. (Luke 4:18)

We are called to do the same because the Bible teaches us to:

'Share each other's burdens, and in this way obey the law of Christ'. Galatians 6:2

CHAPTER FIVE

IT'S THEM, NOT ME!

How to Handle Offence and Blame

'We should be too big to take offence and too noble to give it'.
Abraham Lincoln

When We Take Our Eyes off Jesus

I think that it is pretty safe to say that everyone has had their feelings hurt at some point in their lives. We have all felt the insult of someone else's words or felt a victim due to someone else's behaviour.

Unfortunately, this has been one of the ways that satan has taken *our eyes off Jesus;* because usually when someone hurts our feelings, or who we are as an individual, instead of letting go of their actions we hold on to them, and then resentment begins to build in our souls.

When we have been offended or humiliated, it can bring a deep hurt within, so that within our human nature we want to retaliate. Our view can be:

- *You hurt my feelings—you need to get out of my life.*
- *I'm going to make you pay.*
- *I never want to speak to you again.*
- *You are literally dead to me.*

Sound familiar?

It can seem ridiculous when you read these comments on paper, but I have thought those things, and friendships and even family members have been lost because of the offences I have had. No one is different from the next person, and those views should not be our attitude as Christians.

The Bible says:

> '*...it is to one's glory to overlook an offence*'. Proverbs 19:11 NIV

We should never be tempted to make a permanent decision based on a temporary circumstance. What I mean by this is, strongholds will impact our lives until we deal with the cause.

Therefore, what we deem as a permanent decision (i.e., getting rid of someone from our lives), can change when God's perspective on our reality alters our thinking or reasoning.

We cannot keep offences in our hearts because David reminds us:

> '*If I had not confessed the sin in my heart, the Lord would not have listened*'. Psalm 66:18

Have you ever looked back on times in your life and realised that you were not moving forward? You just felt stuck in your circumstances? Or maybe you could not hear the voice of God clearly? If so, there could be offences that are yet to be dealt with in your life. However, in the Bible, God makes His feelings clear regarding offence.

Please do not get me wrong. I am not trying to make light of any situation where you have been deeply hurt. Things that have happened in your life may have caused deep emotional, spiritual, or even physical scars, but you cannot control the actions of other people.

We can, however, control how we respond to the circumstances we face. That means we should not let other people's faults stop us from walking in freedom. We cannot allow the spirit of offence to ruin our lives and the purpose God has created for us.

The Trap

Offences are used as a trap by satan to hold us from the fullness which God wants us to attain. The devil knows that concealing unforgiveness in our lives can not only stop our progress in becoming more like Christ, but it can delay God's perfect plan for us. Therefore, satan provides the opportunities for us to be offended—regularly!

It can be a believer who has caused the pain. If so, this offends us and feels like disloyalty on their part, I mean, they should know better, right?

David cried:

> *'If an enemy were insulting me, I could endure it; if a foe were rising against me, I could hide. But it is you, a man like myself, my companion, my close friend, with whom I once enjoyed sweet fellowship at the house of God, as we walked about among the worshipers'.* Psalm 55:12-14 NIV

There are those with whom we sit with and sing alongside, or perhaps it is the one who is delivering the sermon. We spend holidays, attend social functions, and share offices with them. Or maybe it is closer; we grow up with, confide in, and sleep next to them. The closer the relationship, the more severe the offence! You find the greatest hatred among the people who were once closest.[36]

My Offence

I became a Christian at the age of 25. Previously, I was married to a man I dated since I was 15. We were married when I turned 20 years old, and divorced by the time I was 21.

He was abusive; and during our time together I became angry and hurt at the pain I went through, emotionally and physically.

I carried so much offence towards him, my friends at the time, and even my family, that my health suffered. I would always want to be the first to tell my side of the story, and of course I blamed everyone for everything. After all, it was them, not me!

Do not mistake what I am saying; no one is to blame for being abused in any way, shape, or form. But sometimes our actions leading up to the incidents may not be the purest. (I am not talking about child abuse). I have now realised this after looking back over the decades of my pain; I could not trust anyone for years. I would have reoccurring nightmares over past hurts, and I continued to make bad decisions that merely ended up spiralling out of control.

Expectations Are Never Met

I no longer think that there is such a thing as a bad relationship or bad marriage (bear with me!) because I believe that hurt people go into relationships or friendships with strongholds that affect their everyday decision-making.

So ultimately their expectations of each other, which are causing offence and eventually bringing devastation to that relationship, can never be met unless they find freedom.

I carried offences towards people from childhood and the accumulation of these built up over time so that I eventually became a recluse.

Kieren one day told me that I needed help because living with me was like living with 'a ghost'. I didn't want to see people or have conversations with others because, being honest, my offences had turned into hate against the world.

Jesus said, *'Offenses will certainly come…'*. Luke 17:1 HCSB

Offences will come no matter how prayerful or faithful we try to be. That means we need to learn what to do when offences do come into our lives.

I attended Elim Ministry Training College at the age of 32, and it wasn't until that point in my life that offence was talked about. All of the strongholds that I had been harbouring for decades came flooding out over that year.

Seeds of the Mind

You see, nothing in life starts big; it is the same with the offence. An offence always begins as a thought, and thoughts are seeds that enter our minds.

These seeds are the beginning developments of offence in our lives that satan uses against us. But *we can refuse* the thought and uproot the seed before an offence is fully grown because then the root becomes bitterness in the garden of our hearts.[37]

Therefore, we must examine our hearts and open ourselves up to God's correction, and also read His Word so that we can discern our thoughts and feelings. The writer of Hebrews urges us:

> *'Look after each other so that none of you fails to receive the grace of God. Watch out that no poisonous root of bitterness grows up to trouble you, corrupting many'.* Hebrews 12:15

On a different note, in Proverbs it says:

> *'The words of the reckless pierce like swords, but the tongue of the wise brings healing'.* Proverbs 12:18 NIV

Sticks and Stones

I cannot begin to tell you how important our words are. They have the power to destroy a person's self-esteem or empower them.

It's Them, Not Me!

King Solomon wrote the book of Proverbs. He was the wisest person to live; and he frequently talks about the tongue for a good reason. The tongue is mentioned more in Proverbs than any other book in the Bible.

I remember my mum saying to me after the endless amounts of bullying throughout my school years, 'Sticks and stones may break your bones, but names will never hurt you'. What a pile of old rubbish that is! I still have a reaction when I hear or read that saying.

Why? Because from personal experience, bruising and even broken bones will heal, eventually, but the words of other people or loved ones can cut so deeply that our lives are changed forever.

One of my darkest times was when I wanted to commit suicide after my first marriage broke up. It was an accumulation of fear, rejection, and feeling worthless. Death seemed like the only way to be free from the heartache of this world.

I remember crying in my room and thinking to myself that I had never asked to be born. I did not choose this life, and I certainly did not want to live in a world where I felt alone.

The Stark Reality

It is said that for every suicide, there are at least 100 suicide attempts.[38] I became one of those statistics because my offence became profound. That is why I am now an advocate for people to not to believe who the world commands them to be, but discover who they are in Christ—because the world is wrong.

Looking back, I thank God that I found Christ because I now understand the vital difference of not being a Christian at that time in my life. Should I have succeeded back when I felt suicidal, my eternity would look very different from where I know I am now going. Due to my hatred towards God and Christianity as an atheist, Heaven would not have been my eternal home.

I have since found freedom from my past, and my health has been restored; but subsequently, I have to fight to stop offence coming back into my life, as we all do.

If we truly love Jesus, then we need to fight to stay free from fault and the lies the enemy tries to make us believe.

I am not perfect, and I do not try to be. I still make mistakes. But I like to think that I try to make the right decisions and think about the consequences of my actions and even the comments I make to others.

Be Brave

Can you imagine if all believers would merely obey Scripture and go and speak to their offenders in the manner Jesus gave us? It would solve many of the problems that exist in the church today. It is essential to talk to the people whom we believe have wronged us for the following reasons:[39]

Most of the time, they are misunderstandings.

Unfortunately for some people, they would instead absorb the offence silently while growing resentful than go and speak to the person to find out what was said. Most of the time, I have found they can be simple misunderstandings. (Philippians 2:3).

It maintains peace within the church.

Whenever there is friction between believers, it can affect everyone. It can obstruct people from entering into worship and receiving God's Word. It can also create an uninviting atmosphere for visitors within the church. (Ephesians 4:1-3).

Evil satan will not be able to outsmart us.

For our spiritual well-being, we must quickly resolve our differences and forgive. Otherwise, satan can hinder our spiritual life and even deceive us into harbouring bitterness or unforgiveness towards others. (2 Corinthians 2:10-11).

It gives accountability.

You do not want anyone to repeat their actions towards you and harm the faith of others. Therefore, confronting their offensive behaviour with love and grace may cause them not to do those things again (Matthew 18:6).

To be able to help someone who has stumbled in his or her faith.

Christians must make every attempt to help the person who has wronged someone, including yourself, where possible, so that they might be reconciled to God. (Read Galatians 6:1).

The Bible does show us how to deal with an offence, and Jesus established a process to be followed in the event of another believer needing correction, following an offence against someone:

> *'If another believer sins against you, go privately and point out the offense. If the other person listens and confesses it, you have won that person back. But if you are unsuccessful, take one or two others with you and go back again, so that everything you*

say may be confirmed by two or three witnesses. If the person still refuses to listen, take your case to the church. Then if he or she won't accept the church's decision, treat that person as a pagan or a corrupt tax collector'. Matthew 18:15-17

1. Go to that person privately. (Matthew 18:15)

If a Christian has done wrong in your eyes or brought an offence against you, Jesus said first to confront them with the issue but remember to keep the matter private between yourselves.

The objective is not to seek justice for a violation against you, but to seek reconciliation with them, and in turn, their return to a right relationship with God.

Why is it important to be kept private?

Because loving others as Christ loves us, requires it. If we are sincerely committed to loving other people as Jesus commands (John 13:34), then even if someone has sinned against us or has done us wrong, we will not want to maliciously injure that person's credibility, as that might hinder their restoration.

For instance, if this person's wrongdoing against you is circulated within the Church, friendship group, or community, but later the person apologises, many people may have already judged this person and the accusations could have damaged people's opinion of the person. Spreading our accusation against an offending party builds a consensus against them and makes it difficult, if not nearly impossible, to then make things right.

Also, many alleged issues between people are a result of misunderstandings. We need first to find out the facts and find out for sure whether what has been said occurred. It's another reason why you are to first go privately to the brother or sister in question and confront them with the alleged offence and hear their side of the story.

Many people foolishly allow themselves to become offended by misinterpreting the other's intentions or listening to rumours and second-hand information, which could contain distortions or exaggerations.

Confronting the offending party and hearing their explanation could immediately resolve many offences. You'd be surprised how many people are so young in their faith that they don't even bother to investigate the facts or hear the other person's side of the story.

Don't forget that there are always three sides to a story: your side, their side, and what the Word of God says. So never assume you know the truth of a matter until you've heard all three.

> *'Humility is the beginning of true intelligence'.*
> **John Calvin**

I could guarantee that there would be far fewer misunderstandings if people did as Jesus instructed. Loving others gives us a desire to believe the best in people, giving them the benefit of the doubt instead of jumping to conclusions and always expecting the worst.

The Bible says:

> *'Love is a safe place of shelter, for it never stops believing the best for others'.* 1 Corinthians 13:7 TPT

If the wrongdoing is proven valid, and the other person asks for forgiveness for the error, we need to express our forgiveness (Luke 17:3-4). Let the matter be resolved, and then do not carry any resentment towards the person.

That's the hard bit; but remember, if they ask for forgiveness and you continue to be full of bitter jealousy…you are held captive by sin. (Acts 8:23)

2. Take another person with you. (Matthew 18:16)

If your attempt fails to resolve the issue, Jesus says you are to take one other Christian and again confront the offending party.

The presence of another Christian is as a witness to strengthen the effect of the confrontation, to encourage people to do what is said in Scripture, to amplify the Lord's presence in the meeting, and to verify the exchange of testimony.

Jesus is not instructing us to bring witnesses to testify against the person who has wronged us but to prove to the exchange between both parties. It is not just about us feeling safer in numbers, but the safety of the numbers. It is the accountability that what is said took place.

3. Tell the church leadership. (Matthew 18:17)

If the first and second attempts fail, Jesus says to then tell it to the church. This doesn't mean the entire church, as this could cause unrest or damage to the faith of young believers. The meaning is that the church pastors or elders are then to bear responsibility in dealing with the person.

Finally, if these three attempts fail, we are no longer required to have an intimate friendship with the person. Although, keep hoping that reconciliation will take place at a later time, and continue to pray a blessing over the person.

What if You Are the Offender?
The Holy Spirit will convict us and generally speaks through our conscience. If this happens, then we should not ignore Him because this is part of what it means to 'walk in the Spirit' (Romans 8).

In other words, if you are aware of anything that you have committed against someone else, then you have a responsibility to go to that person and seek their forgiveness. If you don't, it will hinder your relationship with God and your ability to come freely to pray and worship Him:

> *'Therefore if you bring your gift to the altar, and there remember that your brother has something against you, leave your gift there before the altar, and go your way. First be reconciled to your brother, and then come and offer your gift'.* Matthew 5:23-24 NKJV

Note this Scripture says, *'If your brother has something against you'*. In other words, you might not feel that you have legitimately wronged that person. However, if you are aware that the person harbours an offence against you, you still need to go and try to resolve the issue.

Be willing to be humble to others, even when you don't consider yourself to be at fault. Don't become so self-righteous that you stand in the way of someone reconciling with you or with God (Romans 15:1-3).

Try and offer a sincere apology for any unintentional offence you have caused, and you need to make every effort to resolve the issue with them. Because whether or not the person will forgive you, you have done your part, and therefore you will be blameless in God's eyes.

This section of the chapter is a tough one. I get it. I was always raised that to give in was to show weakness; and it was not until recently that I realised I was still living that lie.

I would openly say, 'I am always right' to the point that my daughter would back me up and say to Kieren, 'Mummy is always right'! Not my proudest parent moment, but as a family, we then worked together in love to show our daughter why I was wrong to say that, and I asked for forgiveness from both Kieren and Sarai.

Do not be afraid to allow the Holy Spirit to reveal any bitterness or anger in your heart. The longer we hide from these things, the stronger they become and ultimately the harder our hearts will grow.

There is a reason that for years my friends used to call me the Ice-Maiden, and it isn't because I love Disney's movie, *Frozen*. My heart was as solid as Ana's stone heart after Elsa had zapped her with her ice powers. I did not want anyone to get close to me. I was angry and bitter about many things in my life, and it turned me cold. I have lived this and seen the magnitude of the effects that it has on people's lives, which is why we need to do what the Bible says in the book of Ephesians:

'Get rid of all bitterness, rage, anger, harsh words, and slander, as well as all types of evil behaviour. Instead, be kind to each other, tender hearted, forgiving one another, just as God through Christ has forgiven you'. Ephesians 4:31-32

Jesus Offended People, so Why Can't We?

The Gospel of Matthew is probably my favourite Gospel because Matthew focuses on what Jesus said and His teachings.

We can read that Jesus did offend some people, but it was purely from the point of obeying His Father and serving others.

His offence did not come from demanding His rights, and that is something that I feel we need to consider with how we approach this in life.

For example, the Pharisees were offended when Jesus healed on the Sabbath. His disciples were offended by the truth His Father had Him preach. Mary and Martha were offended when He delayed His return to heal Lazarus. But you will not find Jesus offending others by serving Himself.[40]

Therefore, if we are going to obey God's ways and be led by the Spirit, we need to understand that we *will offend people*.

Peter sums this up perfectly:

'So then, since Christ suffered physical pain, you must arm yourselves with the same attitude he had, and be ready to suffer, too. For if you have suffered physically for Christ, you have finished with sin. You won't spend the rest of your lives

chasing your own desires, but you will be anxious to do the will of God'. 1 Peter 4:1-2

In other words:

'…If I were no longer preaching salvation through the cross of Christ, no one would be offended'. Galatians 5:11

Paul said that salvation offends people, and that is the truth; the very truth of the Word of God. Therefore, this is the only time we need to stand for what we believe; and without an apology to others.

The Cost of Obeying Christ

In Luke 9:57-62, the Bible talks about the cost of following Jesus. There is always a cost to following Him, and we need to be in the mindset that no matter what that cost is, we will obey what God is asking of us.

Because then, the onus is on God to help us through those difficult times, as it was Him who made that choice for us.

No matter what the offence is, we need to know that God is more significant than the world around us; and although the world is a large place, if we are only focusing on a select few people who have hurt us, then we have made them idols.

God commands to be first in our lives, in the book of Romans it says:

'For although they knew God, they neither glorified him as God nor gave thanks to him, but their thinking became futile

and their foolish hearts were darkened. Although they claimed to be wise, they became fools and exchanged the glory of the immortal God for images made to look like a mortal human being…'. Romans 1:21-23 NIV

There are times when we can make the offence bigger than God, and our offender usually has more influence over our thoughts, actions, and attitude in our day than God does.

Instead, we need to magnify God's love and grace towards us. God is bigger than anything we are facing; and when we know this, then we will be ready to move on and break free from offence.

The Bubbling Pot of 'What's Wrong with Me'?

For me, my biggest problem is when I feel rejected by people with whom I don't have a close personal relationship. It causes uneasy feelings to rise within me like a bubbling pot of black tar, and I find myself taking it out on the people who are close to me, and who love me.

I mean, obviously, I know I am amazing (and modest) but seriously, what do they think is wrong with me? Did I look at them weirdly? Or maybe I said something to offend them?

Sound familiar?

When I start to feel like this, I know I need boundaries. If I have to distance myself from these people to make sure I don't take out my anger on my daughter or my husband, then I will. After all, we can't be friends with everyone.

There are only 24 hours in a day (although I have been known to pray for more) and we need to be careful with how we spend them and with whom we spend them.

Let Go—Life Is too Precious

It's time for us to make sure our lives are spent investing in those we love and whom God has called us to be as individuals, because:

> *'Our days on earth are like grass; like wildflowers, we bloom and die. The wind blows, and we are gone—as though we had never been here'.* Psalm 103:15-16

Life is too precious to hold on to offence.

With all of this being said, we are to love our enemies and pray for those who persecute us! (Matthew 5:44) To love people does not mean pretending that enemies don't exist, or making those enemies your influencers.

When our emotions are determined by how these people treat us, they have gained influence over our lives, and this error needs to be given to God.

This life is a journey and it's not always easy, but God is good, and He will never leave you nor forsake you. (Hebrews 13:5 NIV)

CHAPTER SIX

BROKEN BUT HEALED

How God Uses the Brokenness of Life to Heal Our Soul

'There is no perfection, only beautiful versions of brokenness'.
Shannon L. Alder

You never grow up thinking you are broken or that those closest to us will hurt us. This group can range from our parents, siblings, extended family, friends, teachers, work colleagues, or even our spouse. But from whoever or whenever it occurs, nothing can quite prepare you for the feeling of brokenness and the hopelessness that follows the betrayal of a loved one who was trusted entirely.

The term 'broken heart' is now so widely used within our society that it has become romanticised. I have personally felt broken throughout specific periods of my life, and I can assure you, it is as unromantic as it comes, no matter at what age brokenness strikes.

In those moments of uncontrollable sobbing, ripping the band-aid off (from words or actions used against us) means that brokenness is the kind of pain that commands our full attention because quite frankly, it is like an all-consuming fire.

In a World of Heartbreak

The dictionary defines heartbreak[41] as 'feelings of great sadness or disappointment'; however in today's world, the term brokenhearted usually describes someone who has suffered a failed relationship or the loss of a loved one. The Internet also makes it appear as though almost all heartbreak comes from divorce or failed relationships. But a broken heart may be brought on by an uncountable number of causes such as disappointment in a child's life, loss of a prized possession, or even a job loss, to name a few.

Whatever the cause, the pain of a broken heart can be vast.

If we look at this from a worldly perspective, it generally proclaims that hope is found in therapy and medication. Advice may include taking antidepressants or going on a shopping spree or even getting a makeover. Some advocate the power of positive thinking or that the most common 'cure' is the passage of time.

I am not a medical practitioner and therefore know that there are people who have benefitted from this advice. There can be seasons in our lives when we are advised to take medication; after all, God did create the medical world and the people in that profession.

However, I write this to look at things from a different view. The world's focus is generally a lot different from Christianity's, but we know from the Bible:

'...the Lord looks at the heart'. 1 Samuel 16:7

Therefore, while people may sense a vanishing of the intensity of heartbreak from medication for a short period, compared to their lifetime, only a Christian can experience complete recovery by accessing the power of God, who alone heals the brokenhearted and binds up their wounds. (Psalm 147:3 NIV)

Cosmetic Surgery and Trips to the Spa

Following the end of my first marriage, I decided to do exactly those worldly things. I spent some money I had set aside to buy a house and had cosmetic surgery, because I was told that no one else would love me because I was ugly. I also bleached my hair because apparently 'blondes have more fun'. Got a fake tan and regularly visited the spa. I spent hundreds of dollars each month to ensure that I looked what I deemed as amazing. I created a new me so that, to the world looking in, I would be seen as an overcomer.

I felt like I needed to transform myself, like a trapped butterfly in its cocoon of brokenness, I had to look like I had broken out of the mess.

People said it was as if I had gone fifteen rounds and yet no one could knock me down, metaphorically speaking. I just always seemed to go twice as hard to achieve what I said I was setting out to do.

Therefore, believe me when I say that you can only go a certain length of time before you have to deal with the pain.

I remember that I had an appointment with my doctor because he was trying to persuade me to seek counselling after I had been raped in my early twenties; but being the person that I was at the time, I took the counsellor's business card and thanked the doctor for his advice. However, in my head, I had already shunned this recommendation because *I'll be fine, I'm not weak* and *I can beat this on my own.*

I had the mentality that I could shake those events off, as I had done with other traumatic experiences. It felt comfortable burying hard events that had occurred deep within, and placing them in the too-hard box.

I now know that this was my reaction in order to open 'Pandora's Box' from a lifetime of pain; of being ashamed and feeling broken.

In the previous chapter, I mentioned that Kieren had told me to get help because life for him had become like 'living with a ghost'. The deep ache within us can feel as isolating as a prison cell, and the enemy wants nothing more than to lock us up in that cell of pain and keep us trapped in separation.

But I want to encourage you that God wants the opposite for us because Christ died so that we could live in freedom and that is when I realised that my personality had become a shell of what it once was.

I kept replaying memories over and over. Although I had our daughter to keep me focused during the day, it would take only the slightest sound or even smell to trigger my mind, and I would become a fearful, blubbering mess.

The nights were the hardest, and I remember feeling that I no longer wanted to be trapped inside my nightmares. I did not want to see my life play out in the darkness of my mind and so insomnia became my friend.

Ask for Help, It's OK

In the end, I went to see a Christian counsellor who specialised in neuro-linguistic programming (NLP). He helped me overcome post-traumatic stress disorder (PTSD) that he had diagnosed me with, because it dawned on me that this wasn't just me overreacting. I consequently began to speak to the counsellor about some of the events that occurred in my life.

I started a journey to automatically remember those unpleasant memories in 'a safe, dissociated way'.[42] In other words, I can now speak about those times in my life without becoming a mess. I still remember the events, but I now have a safe emotional distance from them, to not allow them to affect me.

> 'There are many sorts of broken hearts, and
> Christ is good at healing them all'.
> **Charles Spurgeon**

God is the only Physician who can fully heal a broken heart, and He has never failed in His ability to heal anyone who sincerely comes to Him. Sarai, David, Nehemiah, and Hosea all suffered broken hearts for different reasons: an unfertile womb, a shameful trail of sin, desire to be back home, and one-sided love; but God healed them all.

We need to learn to be open and vulnerable with God, which is necessary to let Him heal us. We need to let Him break our hearts in the right way because it is at that time of vulnerability when we can let Him be our refuge and strength. (Psalm 46:1 NKJV)

Beauty from Brokenness

Kintsukuroi is a Japanese art form where broken pottery is mended with lines of gold filigree. The beauty of brokenness is exposed within the pottery because without it the artist would not be able to rebuild the clay into its original design.

Mending the broken pot requires ability, patience, and the loving hands of the crafter. The best thing about Kintsukuroi is that the gold strengthens the weakness and the result is stunning. In fact, it's the brokenness that creates the ultimate strength and thus the beauty of the pot!

Imagine this with the gospel of Jesus Christ.

We were created lovingly in the image of God to be uniquely ourselves. With God's plan and purpose inside every one of us, yet ultimately we are broken due to the corruption of the world that destroys the original design for our lives. Without Christ's redeeming love putting our lives back together over and over again, we can remain in that constant state of brokenness.

But just like me, when we receive His loving embrace and welcome His healing hands of grace, He re-creatively puts us back together again, one piece at a time. It is the golden strand of Christ's restorative and redemptive love that holds us together. I know from my own life that when Christ restores, we are stronger than ever before.[43]

If you are feeling the pain from what you are reading, then I want you to imagine what your life would look like if you saw your brokenness as a chance to grow strong in Christ. To be healed by His love and goodness, rather than merely as something you have to live with.

Can you imagine God using strands of gold to hold all of your brokenness together and then putting each piece into its rightful place? This is then showing not only your metamorphosis of complete beauty and restoration, but also knowing that the Holy Spirit is shining through every crevice of your heart, mind, and soul, radiating through every millimetre of your life for all to see.

I love this Scripture verse from the book of Daniel:

> *'Those who are wise will shine like the brightness of the heavens…'.* Daniel 12:3 NIV

Wisdom comes from transferring the control of your life from yourself to God because wholeness can only come from the One who is filled with unconditional love and unmerited grace.

We need to recognise our lives as overflowing with God's goodness and beautiful design; where we understand God's Kintsukuroi is holding us together.

All of our strengths and brokenness are continuously freed, exchanged, reestablished and transformed for God's glory because He designed only one of us, and that means you are incredibly special to Him. You are not a mistake or here by accident. There is a purpose for your life.

God blesses us to be a blessing for a specific reason, and as children of God we are blessed beyond measure. But we need to choose to utilise those blessings. Living in constant unhappiness and dejection over our fractured lives is like having a million dollars in the bank and living like someone who has become bankrupt.

I certainly never really understood this principle until I started Bible College. That doesn't mean that every person should go and study. Nor was it anyone's fault, as such, as to why the revelation had not come before then: God's timing is perfect after all—but it is true that we cannot use what we do not know, and I had been living in brokenness until that point in my life.

Believing the Lies

One of the lies that I had believed for years was that I was worthless. This was one of the causes of my brokenness, along with rejection.

I believed what the people in my world, as we all tend to do, said about me. There were others who said that I was fat or ugly and useless. Some said that looking at me made them want to retch. And yet, if I gained the courage to try and leave those relationships, I was persuaded to stay, because *no one else would want me.*

I was made to feel disgusting and repulsive even. For short moments when I would look into a mirror at myself, I saw a hideous figure looking back at me. Consequently, at some point, I stopped looking at my reflection; this continued for a long time because of the abuse I received.

So many times I have been asked, "Why?" Why did I stay in those relationships? I could not explain it, and I didn't even try to, even for years afterwards.

But finding out who God indeed was and is and what the Scriptures actually say, meant finding God's truth, and this allowed me to heal. It gave me joy, and I have since been able to process those harsh circumstances because I found freedom.

> **'Brokenness is the bow from which**
> **God launches the arrow of healing'.**
> **Louie Giglio**

Joy doesn't come from our circumstances; it comes from our God. And since God is with us during our trials, it is possible to have joy even in our darkest times.

Joy is in the Lord. Brokenness is in the world. As long as we're alive, both will coexist on earth,[44] but I am no longer ashamed of my story.

I have decided to speak about parts of my testimony in this book to try and help you understand what the web of deceit is doing in your life, and how the venom of lies is slowly taking hold of your soul to destroy God's plan for you. I am a walking testimony of what the world can do and how God overcomes it.

Therefore, I want to discuss what I have learnt after looking back over my abusive relationships, because out of my experience I now feel able, with God's help, to help others who have been in this situation because:

- **I felt responsible.** I was always made to feel guilty about the problems in the relationships. I had been brainwashed for so many years that it was *always my fault* for the beatings and or the criticism.
- **I developed a coping mechanism.** I disconnected during violence to minimise the shock. I knew what was happening, but doing this enabled me to think that he was a good guy really, while the abuse was occurring.
- **I would think of the pain in their lives.** Crazy I know, but I felt sympathy for the people who hurt me. Instead of focusing on their behaviour, I wanted to be there for them, *no matter what*. I would tell myself that I'd do better or I could change, which would then stop the anger. My rationale was, then we'll be happy.
- **I thought they loved me.** I believed that the abuse was just a one-time thing no matter how often it occurred. And I honestly thought deep down, they loved me.

Let God Show You How He Views Brokenness

Let's now go through five different stories within the Bible that show us what we can learn from allowing God into broken things because let's face it, we think of brokenness as messy, but God teaches us differently.[45]

1. Broken pitchers so that the light could shine (Judges 7:18-19)

If we look at this Scripture in Judges 7 in the spiritual sense, then we can understand that the torches represent the Spirit of God, and the pitchers represent our bodies in which the light from the Holy Spirit are often engulfed within. Just like Gideon, God commands us to break the pitcher so that the Holy Spirit will shine brightly from us. If the torch is lit inside of us for too long, then we run the risk of that flame being put out.

It's not just a select few of us who are given the Holy Spirit, but everyone who comes into the knowledge of Jesus and embraces His love and grace.

However, herein lies the problem that so many of us face today; rather than break the pitcher that is keeping the light hidden, we try to hold everything together tightly and do everything in our power to make sure our desires come first, instead of being obedient to God.

This shows us that sometimes there is a need for brokenness, for God to shine through.

2. A broken box so the ointment could be poured out (Mark 14:3)

The breaking of the alabaster box not only anointed Jesus on the day of His burial with perfume, but its fragrance also filled the entire house. It meant that the aroma and blessing came back onto the woman who broke the box.

Whatever we pour out in our commitment to the Lord, and when we bless others with our prayers and love, it will often come back into our own lives and will continue to bring forth a blessing.

When we also live fully committed to God, we will often find that the guidance of the Holy Spirit leads our spirit. Therefore, you will do many things without understanding why you are doing them; you just know that it is what God wants from you.

Alabaster boxes are known for preserving things for an extended period, without losing its quality. Maybe you feel that you have kept something hidden for too long, like a dream or purpose God placed on your heart, and now you fear it has lost its quality; but remember, you are an alabaster box, a perfume waiting to be released. It is never too late.

Once we allow the broken box to release the fragrance of the Lord, it works powerfully for others as a testament and to bring blessings in our own lives.

3. Bread was broken so the hungry could be fed (Matthew 14:19)

Jesus gave thanks for the meal, broke the bread, and gave it to His disciples to give to the crowd. Amazingly, this shows that Christ does not just meet our needs but desires to be extravagant towards us.

God will shatter what little expectations we have if we learn to bring Him what we have already been given. When Christians are willing to offer their lives sacrificially, relinquishing their hold on whatever God has given them in terms of time, money, and talents, God will use these ordinary things to create extraordinary results.

Christians must never believe their resources are too little to serve God. It is remarkable that Jesus fed the people through His disciples. In this way, the disciples had to trust the Lord for everything they distributed. They only gave as they received and God still uses people in the same way today. The problem comes when we tend to doubt that God will fulfil our needs.

The bread needed to be broken to show that God will meet all of our needs, even when we can't see how it will happen.[64]

4. A body was broken so the world could be saved (1 Corinthians 11:24)

This is probably the simplest one to think of. The story of Jesus on the cross tells us that although no bones on Jesus' body were broken, His skin and flesh were torn and broken by blows from rods, by whippings, and by thorns, nails and spears after floggings. Death divided His body and soul, and by that brokenness, we are healed and saved by His blood.

Unfortunately, due to sin entering the world and separating us from the Father, we now partake in suffering and brokenness. This was different for Christ because He was sinless and only broken by the punishment of the cross. He willingly did this for our redemption, so that we could come back into the loving arms of the Father.

Christ's body had to be broken so that you and I could be saved. He was our substitute. Sin started with a man (Adam) and so had to finish with a sinless man (Jesus), or else He would have needed a saviour as well.

5. A broken will so that we will be fulfilled in Christ (Psalm 51:17)

David is a great role model for us of what real heart repentance looks like. He wrote Psalm 51 as a grief-stricken cry to God for forgiveness after his adulterous relationship with Bathsheba and then having her husband murdered to cover up that she'd become pregnant with his baby. David states that there is nothing we can offer God when we have wronged Him, as God only desires true repentance.

Unfortunately, many people miss this. Rather than repent, we try to clean up our act by giving more, praying more, or busying ourselves.

This psalm also points out the one thing God desires more from us than any other: brokenness over our sin. When this occurs, we take the first step toward reconciliation with Him. Repentance is the doorway to freedom in Christ, but satan knows this and will say things like, 'It wasn't that bad compared to...' or, 'God has already forgotten, so there's no need to confess'.

Our will has to be broken because it will naturally go against God. When we listen to the devil's words we remain in captivity. David reminds us that when we acknowledge our wrongs against God, turn from them, and cry out for forgiveness, God promises that He will hear us and forgive (1 John 1:9) so that we remain adopted in Christ.[46]

These five stories in Scripture show that brokenness allows us to seek and grow in the grace and knowledge of our Lord (2 Peter 3:18 NIV) by being transformed and renewing our minds. (Romans 12:2) Sometimes it's not the circumstances we face, but how we choose to meet them that determines our mindset.

The Lies of satan

We must, therefore, face life armed with a real understanding of what it means to walk by faith and not by sight. (2 Corinthians 5:7 ESV) The enemy will come at any opportunity, but are we ready to face him head on? Do we have the strength and courage to call a lie a lie?

The deception through satan should not be able to hold us captive; it's not about what we can see, but about receiving God's supernatural truths which must come by faith.

As believers, we are not defined by past failures, disappointments, or the rejection of others. Our relationship with God and repentance allows us to come back into a right relationship with the Father.

God walks with us through the unique opportunities this life has to offer, including the good times and bad. We can either walk in our strength and what the apostle Paul calls our flesh, or we can walk in the power of the Holy Spirit. The Spirit helps us to overcome our struggles. He is our Helper, our Advocate, our Comforter. (John 14:16 ESV) Ultimately, it is our choice.

It's a hard truth to know that although our circumstances might not change, and God might not fix the fragmented emotions, conditions, or people in our lives, that *we can* still change for the better.[47]

Our natural reaction is to want the pain of the circumstances we face to vanish, but it is more about our character changes. As we draw closer to God, He helps us to overcome, and the peace of God that surpasses all understanding will guard our hearts and minds in Christ Jesus (Philippians 4:7 ESV) in what we have faced or we are currently facing.

Focus on What Matters

How do we focus on the right things? We do this by keeping our eyes on Jesus:

> *'...Because of the joy awaiting him, he endured the cross, disregarding its shame. Now he is seated in the place of honour beside God's throne'.* Hebrews 12:2

Jesus kept His eyes on His Father throughout His suffering, and now He is seated with His Father in Heaven, waiting for His return to earth. Likewise, we too need to keep our eyes focused on Jesus because then we can overcome anything that this world can throw at us.

We can start by focusing on God and giving Him all the glory. We can start by praising Him even when it hurts. Praising God for His goodness, even when things do not make sense.

Would you be willing for God to use your brokenness and your weaknesses for His ultimate purpose?

Would you stand up and be willing to tell others about your shame, your rejection, or even your bitterness?

Christ sees these things as our victories because we are children of God. Would we then be willing to share in those victories before we wear our crown in Heaven?

Human nature goes against this type of thinking. It says we should not speak of the things that have held us back or nearly defeated us. But Paul says in 2 Corinthians that he would:

> '...I am glad to boast about my weaknesses, so that the power of Christ can work through me'. 2 Corinthians 12:9

Each of us is broken in different ways. Our trials and our circumstances are unique; therefore we need to figure out what it looks like for us to overcome our fears, our anxieties, and our battles.

The Bible does not promise to give the answers to specific questions and nor does God; but the Scriptures are given because they are inspired by God and useful to teach us what is right and to make us know what is wrong in our lives. (2 Timothy 3:16 NIV)

In other words, we may have to realign some of our thought processes or myths about what the Bible says, compared to the lies we believe. That is when joy comes. That is the joy that comes from making intentional choices about how we are going to live our lives, despite our circumstances.[48]

Healing Should Be Together

One thing that I have yet to mention is that the pain we feel is personal, but our healing should be communal. An example of what I mean by this is: Has a family member ever gone through a lot of pain but didn't tell you? Isn't it painful when you finally learn about it? And usually for two reasons:
1. It hurts you that they are in pain, and
2. It hurts that you were not trusted to carry their worries alongside them.

As believers, we are called to carry each other's burdens. (Galatians 6:2 NIV) No one would argue that one person couldn't lift more than ten people together. So, why do we often ignore the hands extended to help us carry our burdens? Why do we try to bear that weight on our own?

In our pain, we do have to deal with the most significant portion of that circumstance, but encouragement and support from others within our lives will significantly reduce the burden.

I always used to look to God and say that no one understood me. But people in my church or small group taught me that I was emotionally detached. It was true that I did not like people getting close to me, despite my main 'love languages'[49] being quality time and words of affirmation.

Give me small talk, and I could get away with happily spending an hour or two within the conversation because I was avoiding specific topics. These people, both within the United Kingdom and again in New Zealand, showed me that I knew very little about love, especially God's love, because most of my life had been based on performance and accomplishment, not long-lasting, godly relationships. I was challenged; and in all honesty, I did not like this, as they held me accountable to my words and actions—and still do.

Sometimes we are too comfortable in our pain, our hurts, and challenges from life. It feels familiar, like an old robe that brings comfort when you feel alone, or the childhood toy that takes you back to a time when you felt safe. But pain stops us from having fullness in the relationships that God has brought into our lives.

We become superficial if we only want people to talk about stuff that makes us feel happy. But when we are wrong or missing the point, our trusted friends should be able to confront us in these areas.

At first, I felt badly and guilt-ridden when confronted, but later I learned the freedom that comes from being confronted with love. I found out that people could correct me, because at the same time they could be for me and not against me.[50]

Nothing quite prepared me for when I knew that the strongholds that had continuously surrounded me for most of my life had finally gone. Or that my heartfelt prayers had been answered. The feeling of peace is a strange sensation, at the very least, and complete euphoria, at the most.

That feeling of peace has come to me when God has given me many undeserved miracles in my life. When He has supernaturally surpassed humanity by giving me life-changing events that have held my faith strong ever since.

Humanly speaking, it is impossible. Yet, with God everything is possible, (Matthew 19:26) and I learnt to listen to God, not people. When someone said, 'No', I went to God with prayer and fasting and asked, 'When?'

God's Plan A

It got to the stage where I would often listen to Christians as they would pray for my circumstances or give me a 'word from God'. In my head, I was dismissing what was being said. Instead, at the same time I would be having a conversation with God about what He was actually speaking and thus not listening to them.

I took for granted people in my life because I thought that their advice was secondary compared to God's; but I should have listened to them since God had given them wisdom for my circumstances. I did not know at that time that God created us for a relationship. Relationship with Him, but also a relationship with others as well! Hence why God tells us to:

'Love each other. Just as I have loved you...'. John 13:34

We are to show the same love and kindness to all the people God brings into our lives so that we can uplift each other in the bad times and rejoice in the good.

> *'When you walk with God, you will walk more closely with each other'.*
> **Adam Cappa**

I believe now that the joy and satisfaction we experience in life is tied directly to the quality of relationships we possess with other people, especially when God is the Foundation and Jesus the Cornerstone of our faith. They bring stability in an unstable world, and God's Word never changes.

For instance, you can be hugely successful in your business, and yet if your marriage goes wrong, the satisfaction of life can leave you. You may own a beautiful house, but if you do not get along with your neighbours, you will no doubt experience anxiety and stress within your home.

Our relationship with God often plays an essential role in our relationships with Him and other people. This reality is often overlooked. John speaks of this seeming disconnect:

> *'If someone says, "I love God," but hates a fellow believer, that person is a liar; for if we don't love people we can see, how can we love God, whom we cannot see? And he has given us this command: Those who love God must also love their fellow believers'.* 1 John 4:20-21

We cannot just love God and not others.

I am a twin, and I will talk about this more in the next chapter, Do You See Me?, but because I always had competition, I wanted God to myself. This meant that my faith became performance-based. Could I make God prouder of me than other people? This was merely another lie that I had believed, as in reality; I didn't want to share *my God*. My relationship with my heavenly Father had been superceded by how I viewed my earthly family.

So when I read the following verse within Ephesians, it struck me like never before:

> *'He makes the whole body fit together perfectly. As each part does its own special work, it helps the other parts grow, so that the whole body is healthy and growing and full of love'.*
> Ephesians 4:16

It was not *just people doing it. It was God Himself!* God was working directly through people when they were helping me.[51] We need to battle brokenness with heartfelt praise, loneliness with community, and discouragement with God's Word.

When we surround ourselves with God's people, we will see that healing does take a village, and the village is stronger for it. We must combat resounding pain with unwavering worship to the Father, alongside each other so that we can pray together. That is God's Plan A for humanity.

Although we may be broken, we are healed through other Christians and Christ Himself.

CHAPTER SEVEN

DO YOU SEE ME?

How to be Uniquely You in a Comparison-Frenzied World

'Comparison is the thief of joy'.
Theodore Roosevelt

Comparison is ugly, and yet it seems unavoidable in the world today. So many people, including myself, suffer from being compared to others, which become some of the most destructive strongholds in our lives. It is not ok to compare anyone so that they feel belittled or of lesser value than God places on them. I write this chapter to address some of that ugliness and replace it with God's truth.

Compared Since Birth

I mentioned in the previous chapter that I am a twin; and although this chapter is on comparison and ultimately not about me being a twin, I still wanted to give you a brief outline so you can see where I am personally in all of this. I understand the struggle of comparison and the feeling of rejection from having dealt with these things within my own life.

Firstly, people seem to ask the same questions, so I thought that I would confirm what most people frequently want to know about twins:

- No, we are not identical (he is 6 ft 3 ins/192cms tall, and I am…not that tall).
- He is the oldest by three minutes (and he never lets me forget it).
- No, we don't finish each other's sentences.
- No, we can't read each other's minds.
- No, there is no 'evil' twin (although if there were, it would be him, obviously!).
- Yes, twice, only twice in my life, have I felt pain when he was hurt.
- And lastly, no, I actually do not like being a twin. (#shock-horror) And yet that never stopped anyone from comparing us throughout our childhood.

My parents (our mum) would consistently dress us in the same type of outfits to make sure people would know we were twins.

As twins, we were scrutinised most days, and this was a big reason as to why I hated being one. It ranged from our appearance, to exam results, to life decisions. Twins seem to be constantly compared; and therefore it can seem as though they are always walking in each other's shadows.

I lost count of the number of people who said, 'I wish I had a twin'. Maybe they did, but to be honest, unless you are a twin, you have no idea what it's like. People have this fascination with the idea of twins, triplets, etc., but the reality is so much more complicated than you can imagine—because we are individuals. Think about being compared to someone you might feel is nothing like you, daily.

Most people in the world look for ways to be an unique individual in how we present ourselves. We want to shine, to stand out, to be noticed; and unfortunately, most want to be validated in this social-media-frenzied world.

I suffered from rejection from a very young age. This got worse as I became older after being told that my brother was 'the favourite' by different people in our lives.

At an impressionable age, it kind of messes with your mind; and this, unfortunately, led me to make decisions that had consequences in the desire to feel wanted.

I blamed my parents and I blamed my twin. 'It's their fault'; but actually it was mine. I was looking for validation in all the wrong places. They only lived as they knew how to live. I talk about *expectation* in the next chapter, but while on this journey with God, He has shown me that generally, humans do not like to be compared to the next person.

Yet the world seems to constantly be in a state of comparison, which ultimately leads to the feeling of rejection. We can then develop an 'I need to be seen as better than you' mindset.

Needing Validation

No one should feel alone in this world and no one should feel like they have to compare themselves or others to anyone to feel better.

Love should have no labels. No hashtags. You are uniquely you. God created only one of you for a reason; and ultimately, I cannot do what God intended for you to fulfil in this world. And yet, we are always looking at the next person and asking, 'Why her?' Or 'Why him?'

We even tend to stalk these people on social media (don't say you haven't) to see if they have more 'likes' or more 'followers'. Even to the point of how successful they seem in the world. But then we ask the question that is really on our minds, *'Why not me?'*

Validation is what the devil keeps on our minds to stop us from seeking what truly matters, which is meaningful relationship with God and with others.

We seem to forget that there can only be one Steven Furtick or only one Kylie Jenner. Whether they are Christians or not, we all desire, yearn, want, covet, strive, or whatever you want to call it, to be like other people in some way.

How many of us have prayed to God things like: 'Please Lord, let me glorify You by doing...for me', or even, 'Give me more followers on social media so I can bring people to Your name'. Or maybe, 'Give me endless amounts of money to serve You better, so I can be a blessing to others'.

Whatever our desires are, it seems that we are all looking for one thing—to be seen in this world.

> *'Oh, don't worry; we wouldn't dare say that we are as wonderful as these other men who tell you how important they are! But they are only comparing themselves with each other, using themselves as the standard of measurement. How ignorant'!* 2 Corinthians 10:12

I know the comparison game well. I have played it many times, whether it was comparing my fashion style to my friends', comparing my child's behaviour to those kids who seem like Jesus Himself, or comparing my follower count on social media. I have played this game often and lost every time; and you thought you were the only one.

> ***'We won't be distracted by comparison
> if we are captivated with purpose'.***
> **Bob Goff**

We Are All Unique, Not Equal
Often in our own attempt to want everything to be fair, we can be tempted to think that God loves us equally, and therefore our lives should look the same as those with whom we are comparing ourselves.

However, to say that God loves us equally is flawed, because the word 'equal' implies that His love can be measured, and it cannot. The same would mean for us to be replaceable with each other, but we are not because God's heart is not divided into compartments. No one else can take the place of you or me, hence why I said earlier, that there is only *one of you*. God does not love you equally because He loves you uniquely.[52]

The Real Reason We Compare

The comparisons we have in our lives reveal our brokenness. The reason we compare ourselves is that deep inside we are disappointed with the hand we have been dealt in life and who we are as individuals.

Whether we feel good or bad after we compare ourselves to someone else, we do it because things aren't right inside us. This means that ultimately, it is a heart issue.

Comparison is the grief of subconsciously admitting that we are not satisfied with how God has made us. We are not happy with where He has placed us in this world, and that we don't appreciate the life He has predestined for us. Comparing ourselves to others means that we do not trust that God has the best intentions for us. We think we know better; but actually, comparison lies about who we indeed are.

Think about it. Do we have anything to compare if we identified ourselves as being truly unique or even being one of a kind?

> *'You saw me before I was born. Every day of my life was recorded in your book. Every moment was laid out before a single day had passed'.* Psalm 139:16

I want to get vulnerable about myself for a second.

One thing that I still struggle with periodically is comparing my body to others. I was severely bullied, and I was told that I was too fat, so I innocently skipped a meal here and there to lose the odd pound or two. But it became a vicious cycle, and I ended up developing an eating disorder during my primary school years.

The sad thing is, this can still affect how I see myself today.

The years of torment, which I spoke briefly on in the previous chapter, meant that I became prideful in comparing myself to others.

Deep down I loved to be called 'pretty' and 'skinny' because that was what gave me a temporary inner joy compared to all of the pain that I had endured. When someone said those things to me, it was worth it, until that split second when the enemy told me what they said was a lie, as then I strived to do better. I now understand that this was a period in my life when I believed all that the enemy told me I was, rather than who God says I am.

How many of us still find it easier to believe the hurtful things rather than the life-giving truth of Christ?

> *'But now I'm afraid that just as Eve was deceived by the serpent's clever lies, your thoughts may be corrupted and you may lose your single-hearted devotion and pure love for Christ'.* 2 Corinthians 11:3 TPT

The Rich and Famous Versus Me
The worst period of my life for comparison seemed to come after I gave birth. The way my body changed was something that I fought within my mind, constantly.

Not because I didn't want to be pregnant, but stretchmarks, varicose veins, and cellulite, to name a few, was not part of the deal for me to be pregnant! Continuously comparing myself to all the rich and famous, I would read all the magazines that reported not two weeks after giving birth, these 'perfect' women were back in their pre-pregnancy clothes and looking radiant.

Like, WHAT?

As for me, I looked down and saw, even eighteen months on, the brutal aftermath of birth. I developed post-natal depression, and I became too afraid to talk about what I saw as 'my inadequacies' to anyone. I had a fear of being rejected as a good mother.

I needed to be perfect, right? Everyone else seemed to be!

I would scroll through social media and see everyone's 'perfect lives'. Their perfect babies, perfect un-messy, clutter-free homes—everything was perfectly perfect! I felt like a mess compared to them, and I felt inadequate, insufficient, and unworthy to be loved.

We all know that life is chaotic to some degree. And in truth, everyone's lives are far more complicated than we will ever get to see on their social media pages, so why do we forget this? Why is it that when we look at our phones or iPads, we become so detached from that reality?

I got to the stage where I was tired of feeling like I needed to compete. I became so low that I even felt like Kieren could do better. Nowadays, those thoughts are thrown in the trash where they belong, but I always desired to be 'more'. I was never totally satisfied with what was happening at that time in our lives. I was always worrying about how I looked; therefore, I was always looking to the next thing to help me achieve it all.

> *'That is why I tell you not to worry about everyday life—whether you have enough food and drink, or enough clothes to wear. Isn't life more than food, and your body more than clothing'?* Matthew 6:25

Keeping Up with the Joneses

Like the Israelites, we grumble and complain and say that the manna God gives us every day is tasteless, the water of life we drink isn't refreshing, and we'd rather be back in Egypt, enslaved and under a heavy yoke.[53]

My whole life, I had competed with my twin, whether he realised it or not, and then with all the unhealthy relationships I had. I always felt like I needed to be keeping up with the Joneses.

The Cambridge English Dictionary defines this term well:

> 'To always want to own the same expensive objects and do the same things as your friends or neighbours, because you are worried about seeming less important socially than they are'.[54]

Then one day Kieren got down on his knees and kissed the stretch marks on my stomach. I burst into tears, trying to pull away, but he held me tight. He told me that these battle scars on my body were a memory of something beautiful. Of a journey, that we had taken together and had won a great victory with God because the world told us that journey was impossible.

My battle scars were perfection in my husband's eyes. When I saw ugliness, he saw beauty. When I saw heartache from the comparison, he saw radiance from individuality. He saw the conqueror in me; and just like Christ, Kieren loved me at my darkest.

> *'But Christ proved God's passionate love for us by dying in our place while we were still lost and ungodly'!* Romans 5:8 TPT

Comparison takes away our joy because it makes us forget the blessings we have and it leads us to complain against God. That then eventually turns us into self-focused, unhappy, and disheartened individuals.

Just like me, I believed only the negative. Someone could have given me one hundred compliments, and I would have rejected everyone in my head. Yet if someone insulted me, just once, I believed every word said, because I was not grounded in the love of Christ, I was grounded in ME!

> *'The thief's purpose is to steal and kill and destroy. My purpose is to give them a rich and satisfying life'.* John 10:10 NLT

> **'No one can make you feel inferior without your consent'.**
> ***Eleanor Roosevelt***

Our True Identity

While comparing ourselves to others may distract us from the real issues going on, it doesn't heal us or even deal with the sin in our lives. The only way we can break free of this comparison trap is by finding our hope and identity in Christ.

Those who know the saving power of Christ have been given a whole new identity. No longer are we destined for eternal hell. We have been given a new standing, a new name, and a new destiny.[55]

> *'But you are not like that, for you are a chosen people. You are royal priests, a holy nation, God's very own possession. As a result, you can show others the goodness of God, for he called you out of the darkness into his wonderful light'.* 1 Peter 2:9

When you know whose you are, you know what is available to you. Your concept of God will be reflected in you. Your God perceptions will ultimately be reflected in the life you live and the choices you make.[56]

No longer am I the girl whose identity rests in where I live, what I do, or who I am. Those are artificial conditions, and my heart no longer lives there.

Instead, my heart now rests in the fact that I have been adopted into the family of God, have been rescued from the fate of hell, and will live with Jesus forever.

God commands us to be strong and courageous. (Joshua 1:6) Strong, so that we can fight to become victorious in this world, and not be afraid; and courageously knowing that whatever God has for us, it is good. And most of all, He loves us in all circumstances.

> *'...all that Jesus now is, so are we in this world'.* 1 John 4:17 TPT

When we read the Scripture in 1 John, an eternal connection is made, and the gap between His restoration and errors in our truth, meet. We are positioned to identify with who God says we are. This should bring an understanding and revelation of who Christ is to us because God has placed us for all of that as well!

Who do you see Jesus as?[57] For instance, I know:
- *Because* He is love, I am loved, and I can love.
- *Because* He is life, I am alive.
- *Because* He is able, I am capable.
- *Because* He is my brother, I am God's daughter.
- *Because* He is Almighty, I am mighty.
- *Because* He is the Healer, I am healed.
- *Because* He is Wisdom, I am wise.
- *Because* He is who He is, I am who He says I am.[58]

Comparison robs us of joy and leads us away from Jesus. We need to stop looking to others to feel good about ourselves; because when we look to others for affirmation, we will always feel as though we are on the outside looking in. Instead, look to Christ who gives joy, peace, and love that surpasses any situation.

There is no lifetime achievement, social media post, or any single person who can ever write with assurance the words God alone can inscribe on your heart:[59]

'Loved, beautiful, valued, intimately known…mine.'

God made you to be YOU, not a duplicate of someone else.

'By the grace of God I am what I am…'. 1 Corinthians 15:10 NIV

There are four ways to stop comparing ourselves to others and find peace and happiness in being who God created us to be. If we all walked in our true identities, the enemy would have very little to do in this world!

This is the only time in *Life's Greatest Battles* that I felt the need to write prayers at the end of each section because the subtitle to this book is *'Awareness Is the Start of Breakthrough"*; and therefore, I don't want us to move past this without giving our circumstances, regarding comparison, to God:[60]

1. Remember that you are fearfully and wonderfully made.
Psalm 18:30 tells us God's ways are perfect; and Psalm 139:14 tells us that we are *'fearfully and wonderfully made'*. Therefore, we are God's unique creation. As we surrender our hearts and will to Him, He can mould us and transform us into precisely who He wants us to be. So when we begin to feel inadequate and feel the temptation to compare, He brings truth into our souls.

Prayer:

> *Thank You, Father, for making me the way I am. I pray that You will transform my thinking and the way I feel inside, to see Your goodness shining through me. Father, I ask that You will show me the desires of Your heart for my life. Thank You that there is no reason to compare myself because only I can fulfil all that You created me to be, in Your perfect plan. Amen.*

2. Know that we all have different strengths and weaknesses.

No matter how hard you and I try, someone will always be better at that something than we are. So when we start feeling the need to compare, we must recognise our opportunity to practice humility. This too can come through a simple prayer.

Prayer:

> *Thank You, Lord, that in my weakness You are strong. Help me to rely on You, rather than seek out someone who appears weaker than me, to make myself feel stronger. Thank You, Father, that I no longer need to look to others but only to Your guidance to bring Your truths to my life so that I can discern the lies of the enemy, to show who I really am in You. Amen.*

3. Choose compliments over comparison.

When you notice a parent who can manage their child or children in public better than you may be at that time, don't start thinking of the many reasons why they are probably able to do that. I mean, obviously, they must be rich, so can bribe their kids with state-of-the-art gadgets, rather than extra screen time that your child might be bribed with. Or someone you know can do something well that you have struggled with, or they get recognition, and you don't. Instead of getting jealous, compliment them.

I once saw a woman at a conference wearing the same top I was wearing. Rather than dwell on that and begin to hate her for it, I quickly said, 'You have amazing taste'. The sincere smile on my face killed the previous drive I would have had to make myself feel better. Genuinely complimenting others outwardly keeps us from complaining secretly and cultivating a critical spirit.

Prayer:

> *Father, help me to see others as You created them to be. Let there be no comparison or fear of rejection; rather, enable me to show the love of Christ to all. Show me how to be the light in the darkness and shine Your goodness in the world. Help me to be sincere and caring to those who are in my life. Thank You, Jesus, that Your mercy and grace is undeserving, yet You give it freely. Enable me to do the same. Amen.*

4. Rely on God's opinion rather than the opinion of others.

Our insecurity often causes us to compare ourselves with others, looking for a way to feel superior. But what if you and I relied on God's opinion of us before we had a chance to listen to our own, or others' opinions?

If someone is praising a person who hasn't done half of what you've done, quietly thank God that He sees your heart and actions. He knows the real story; and that's all that matters.

Prayer:

> *Lord, help me to be content with Your evaluation of me over anything else. Tell me what to think when my opinions of others, or even myself, get in the way. Keep my mind from going in the wrong direction. Father, help me to see that it is not my ways, or that of others, which I should desire to live by, but only by the example of Jesus. Amen.*

As we focus on the cross, we cannot but help see the love of God for our lives. We need to be genuinely thankful for whom God has made us to be and what purpose He has for others and us. This alone eliminates comparison and rejection because we become confident in *our identity*.

We are established based on what Christ did for us rather than what we need to do. We have the power of choice, which gives us control over how we react to situations in our lives. We cannot control what happens to us or even what people say, but we can certainly choose how we respond.

Circumstances will help us to become more like Christ. Trials will come. But after all is said and done, there will be eternal rewards for those who put loving God first in their lives.

> *'God blesses those who patiently endure testing and temptation. Afterward they will receive the crown of life that God has promised to those who love him'.* James 1:12

When I am seeking justification…when I am trying to be seen in this world…I want to learn how to not want validation from other people. I do not want to compare. Nor do I want to feel the pain of rejection through being compared.

Instead, I want to learn how to run to God no matter what life throws at me. I want to run into His arms like a prodigal son returning home, because I know where I belong. I pray you now know that too.

As Christians, our identity is found in Christ alone, and therefore rejection is merely a momentary bump in the road; feeling of an unworthy feeling. If someone is strong enough to bring me down, then I am going to show them that I am strong enough to get back up. I love the lyrics from this song sung by Frank Sinatra:

> 'Now nothing's impossible, I've found for when my chin is on the ground, I pick myself up, dust myself off, and start all over again. Don't lose your confidence if you slip, be grateful for a pleasant trip, And pick yourself up, dust off, start over again. Work like a soul inspired until the battle of the day is won'.[61]

I want to find security in God's embrace because I know that when my heart is overwhelmed, He needs to be my core. He needs to be the Rock on which I find rest.

He needs to be my beginning and my end. Jesus is the only One who can give us peace, a feeling of peace that surpasses all understanding (Philippians 4:7) because He is our Rock of safety.

> 'From the ends of the earth, I cry to you for help when my heart is overwhelmed. Lead me to the towering rock of safety, for you are my safe refuge, a fortress where my enemies cannot reach me'. Psalm 61:2-3

I choose to claim my heritage as a child of God and move forward in grace, which is the gift given freely by Jesus. If we do not know our heritage, then the bumps in the road will take us out, but the opportunity to know Jesus on a deeper level should be our primary focus. It is our highest honour as a child of God to know and begin to understand our Lord.

Therefore, when we reach for our phones or gadgets to see what other people are doing, rather than choosing to know Him more, we have actually chosen the lesser thing. It is far better to know God than to be known by man.[62]

To put it simply, comparison and rejection are not of God. Thus, they should have no place in our hearts. There should be no contest or striving in this world because we are all here to do one thing; serve Christ until we see Him again.

So the question I asked in the title of this chapter: Do you see me?

Maybe I don't. Perhaps even the world doesn't know your name. Maybe the world never will. But God does, and that is the most important thing.

That is the only thing that truly matters.

> 'Am I now trying to win the approval of human beings, or of God? Or am I trying to please people? If I were still trying to please people, I would not be a servant of Christ'. Galatians 1:10 NIV

CHAPTER EIGHT

THE ATOMIC BOMB

Why Expectation Leads to Guilt and Shame

'Expectation is the root of all heartache'.
William Shakespeare

The Introverted Conversations

Our expectations are not always correct in life because there are actually flaws in our logic and thinking. Now I know that might come as a shock to some, but this also includes things like the predisposition of our hopes and dreams and even the desires of our hearts.

Therefore, I knew that this chapter was vital in finding freedom within our walk with Christ, just because there are so many who still hold on to guilt and shame but also carry the expectations of loved ones.

Whether we like to admit it or not, we can be hopeless romantics. But we can also concoct an array of situations within our mind of

The Atomic Bomb

how life, relationships, and even how our career aspirations would go if we could write the novel of our 'Life Achievements'.

Are you the type of person to have conversations with people in your head? I don't mean like schizophrenia, but more that you have disagreements with people you know in your mind, say after an argument has taken place or maybe you failed to stick up for yourself at work?

Our mind is a place where we become victorious. And let's face it, in this moment, it seems to be the only time when we will stand up for ourselves!

We become loud and proud as we replay those events over and over until we say, or do, the right thing to bring that look of 'the cat who got the cream' on our face.

Are you the introvert who would usually turn away from confrontation and yet in your head you suddenly become the most eloquent individual that this world has ever seen? No more are you a bumbling mess as you try to stand up for yourself; no, siree! Because in your mind you imagine situations like:
- You have just annihilated your 'friend' who keeps making you look weak in front of all your peers.
- You have just stood up to a family member who has bullied you all your life.
- You have just conquered a fear.
- Your manager, who has never even said hello to you, has just given you that pay rise you have deserved for the past five years—just because.

...But reality then hits, and you realise that these scenarios are all in your mind.

Or is it only me?

I have had these remarkable conversations many times, but I have also found in doing so—apart from the unrealistic scenarios—it caused an expectation to be created in my life. Each one brought a belief system that I then lived by with how I felt and even how I would react to a particular individual or circumstance.

The Problem with Having Expectations

In our dreams for life, up until a certain point, we will always want a 'happily ever after', and yet life rarely ends with *Prince Charming* carrying us off into the sunset on his white steed.

So why do we form impulsive expectations so easily?

Why is it, when beliefs are not met, pain arises, and we often place the blame on that something or someone who does not live up to our expectations; even if they were irrational, to begin with?

I spoke about this scenario briefly in a previous chapter, but I often hear of people's marriages that have run into problems. It's not the marriage that is the problem. It is the individuals who have the issues and have come into the marriage without realigning expectations of themselves or their partner.

Perhaps they found it too hard to deal with the past, as I did.

The Atomic Bomb

That is where the real problem lies and why expectations based on human values alone can cause so much pain and trouble, not only for the individuals but also for others as well.

For example, let's use the scenario of when a man and a woman get married, they both can carry expectations into the marriage.

The man may assume that his wife will cook and clean and mainly do everything for him, just as his mother did.

The woman might think that she will have 2.5 kids, a dog, and a house with a white picket fence; but actually, her husband expects her to work, and he only wants one child and to live in the city.

This couple is now facing resentment, bitterness, and sometimes pride because these things were based entirely on what *they hoped for*. They expected a particular outcome and those expectations weren't met.

No promises were made by the man or woman, and yet both can feel as if they had been deceived, lied to, or even tricked into the relationship. This can bring environments where they feel they would never have entered into the lifelong commitment because 'He's not the person I married!' Or, 'She's not the person I married!'

Many times, expectations come from what we're used to: our family growing up, or even our personalities. If you grew up in a family where shouting and open conflict was the usual way to resolve a problem, you would be a person who would expect others to yell and be confrontational if they had a problem with you.

Alternatively, if you are a person who prefers to disguise your emotions and talk your issues out rationally, you may find it impossible to convince the person who is argumentative that you have been hurt emotionally, physically, or spiritually, because you are not shouting at them and should not have to in order to resolve any issues.[63]

This is just one of many expectations we can have.

Yet the Bible sets out some core values that can help us form beneficial expectations and also deal with the expectations we have of others.

Communication

How many people can say that we are open and honest with ourselves and with others in the first instance? We all fail others and ourselves in many ways:

> 'Indeed, we all make many mistakes. For if we could control our tongues, we would be perfect and could also control ourselves in every other way'. James 3:2

We should, therefore, be able to admit when we are wrong and we should not base our expectations on mere theories but the truth of God:

> 'Spouting off before listening to the facts is both shameful and foolish'. Proverbs 18:13

We should discuss with our loved ones what our expectations are and what theirs are of us. I can look back now and see that most of my disagreements in life have come from either miscommunication or unrealistic expectations, and this then allows me to (hopefully) realign my belief system with Christ.

Forgiveness

The people in Jesus' day were expecting the Messiah to come soon. (Luke 3:15)

However, when He came, they had some unrealistic expectations. They wrongly hoped for Jesus to establish His kingdom there and then:

> *'The crowd was listening to everything Jesus said. And because he was nearing Jerusalem, he told them a story to correct the impression that the Kingdom of God would begin right away'.* Luke 19:11

When He did not fulfil the expectations they had, they became frustrated enough to kill Him and release a convicted murderer instead. But Jesus forgave as this verse shows us:

> *'Jesus said, Father, forgive them, for they don't know what they are doing…'.* Luke 23:34

If Jesus could forgive the men who called out, 'Crucify Him'! Surely we can forgive our loved ones and friends who have incorrect expectations of us.

Love

Love is patient and it is kind and it definitely does not insist on its own way! This passage in Scripture is well known even amongst the hardest atheist because it is used so often in marriage ceremonies or memorabilia.

> *'Love is patient and kind. Love is not jealous or boastful or proud or rude. It does not demand its own way. It is not irritable, and it keeps no record of being wronged. It does not rejoice about injustice but rejoices whenever the truth wins out. Love never gives up, never loses faith, is always hopeful, and endures through every circumstance'.* 1 Corinthians 13:4-7

Paul's intention for these verses was so that the Church would know that although we all have different giftings and abilities; love is available to everyone.

Fearless Love

We need to remember that God created us to be different from each other.

If we have formed expectations of friends or loved ones that they cannot live up to, it is not their fault.

God gives us the power to change our expectations; and if we find that our expectations of others are unreasonable, we might have to be flexible.

We are called to love as God loves us, (John 13:34) which means to love a person without expectation. To love them fearlessly, fearless of being hurt, fearless of being vulnerable, fearless of being unashamedly in love with God, and everyone else in our lives.

We should not be afraid of going 'all out' within our relationships because fearless love is not based on the performance of a person but the loving faithfulness of God.[64]

Being fearful of love is not from God. For instance, when disappointments arise, do you place walls around your heart because you are afraid of 'what if'? That is worldly love.

> '*God will never give you the spirit of fear...*'. 2 Timothy 1:7 TPT

What God desires for us is having fearless love in Christ. This is what we received from Him when He was writing our names within His Book.

He can name every star in the sky, (Psalm 147:4) in every galaxy, known and unknown, and yet He decided that He needed *only one of you* in this world.

His love for you comes with no expectation, no consequence, no resentment, and no unkindness, because God is love.

Love is fearless because God is fearless.
We are God's, so we can love fearlessly.

We need to understand that we are positioned to love just as fearlessly when we receive God's fearless love. Because those who love fearlessly, live fearlessly.[65]

Do Die

I am part of Hope Centre New Zealand, which is a fantastic Spirit-led church. Our senior pastor, Luka, will often say, 'We DO die'. This declaration comes out of the following Scripture:

> *'If any of you wants to be my follower, you must give up your own way, take up your cross, and follow me'.* Mark 8:34

When you are a disciple of Christ, it requires obedience. Jesus did not mean that we should seek out pain intentionally from this Scripture, but He was talking about the courageous effort needed to follow Him moment by moment. To do His will, even when the work asked of us is difficult and the future is not yet known.

Can you love the unlovable people in your life without expectation?

Can you show reckless love to others, even if you think they don't deserve it?

Jesus loves me in spite of my past and even my current mistakes. The actions I have done. The things I have said. He loves me, without question.

Jesus showed us from the parable of the lost sheep (Matthew 18:12-14) that He will always go out searching for the one and leave the ninety-nine because the one sheep that is alone is the one in actual danger.

Do you love your life more than that of other people?

Jesus told the Pharisees that:

> *'There is more joy in heaven over one lost sinner who repents and returns to God than over ninety-nine others who are righteous and haven't strayed away'!* Luke 15:7

At Hope Centre, 'We DO die', because Jesus didn't worry about the accusations of others, as He wanted to bring the gospel of God's kingdom to the 'lost sheep': people considered beyond hope.

So just as Jesus would have died for the one, we too should be willing to do the same. Can we indeed lay down our lives to help the poor, the needy, the broken and the lost?

Take Up Our Cross

Fearless love is the kind that goes against our natural inclinations, which is why Jesus said we must *take up our cross*. It helps us to remember that we must set aside our desires and instincts so that we can give away such things as love while expecting nothing in return.

At the time when Paul wrote his first letter to the church in Corinth, the city was morally corrupt, and love had become mixed-up with little meaning.

But, as I wrote, Paul addresses this when he writes on love in 1 Corinthians 13. Yet, to me, John sums up love nicely by saying that love is the greatest of all our virtues, as it is the attribute of God Himself:

> *'But anyone who does not love does not know God, for God is love'.* 1 John 4:8

Loving others without expectation involves a selfless life. It shows others that you care! It's not about the rules. It's not about keeping the law like the Pharisees tried to do. Jesus came to fulfil the law by showing that He loved us so much; He died so that we may live!

Think of it like this:

If you believe in Christ, then faith is the foundation and content of God's message.

Hope is the attitude we live by; so from this, love is the action from which we then minister.

When faith and hope are in line with Christ, you are free to love entirely because you understand how God loves you. In everything, we should look to God and trust Him because He never disappoints us:

> 'Trust in the Lord with all your heart; do not depend on your own understanding'. Proverbs 3:5

God's promise should be our only expectation in life. We know that He will fulfil His Word because He has done it before when Jesus was raised from the dead. We have read it and believe it:

> 'Not a single one of all the good promises the Lord had given to the family of Israel was left unfulfilled; everything he had spoken came true'. Joshua 21:45

Therefore, we can expect God to do precisely what He says is to come:

> '...through the power of these tremendous promises you can experience partnership with the divine nature, by which you have escaped the corrupt desires that are of the world'.
> 2 Peter 1:4 TPT

When based on God's Word, our expectations will never fail to be met because God's Word is perfect in every way...His laws lead us to the truth, and His ways change the simple into wise. (Psalm 19:7)

Having an expectation in God can be an amazing experience. He alone can bring the revelation we need to endure while we wait for the Lord's return:

> 'We look forward with hope to that wonderful day when the glory of our great God and Saviour, Jesus Christ, will be revealed'. Titus 2:13

We need to encourage each other to fight for the faith that God has given to each of us, rather than expect something from each other because only God can provide what we need. (Philippians 4:9)

We need to remember that when we put an expectation on other people or ourselves instead of on God, it will only lead to disappointment, guilt, and even shame in their lives (and even ours) because those expectations can never be met.

We will *never* meet up to other people's expectations and nor should we have to. But the result from the pressure to conform can run so deep that we then only see failure in our lives or in the very fabric of our identity rather than the freedom that Christ gave to us through the resurrection.

> *'The less we talk about shame,*
> *the more control it has over our lives'.*
> *Brené Brown*

Living with Guilt and Shame

I want to speak about guilt and shame for the rest of this chapter because this was the root of my existence for a very long time. It stopped me from walking in the purpose that God has for me as a daughter of the Most High, even after I found Christ. As mentioned at the beginning of this chapter, it seems that many of us suffer from guilt and shame in some way.

How many of us know the difference between guilt and shame, let alone how it starts to work in our lives? Let me explain…

Life to me felt like hard work, and it had certainly not been a bed of roses at times. I remember crying, alone in my bedroom, after being told for the countless time, that my parents wished they had swapped me at birth.

I felt like my life was out of control. A never-ending storm that eventually became more like a hurricane, devastating everything in its path.

I decided that everyone would be much better off without me as I obviously made them miserable—my very existence became my most profound failure.

The Atomic Bomb

I do not even remember when my despair turned into the need to control my circumstances. At some point, I decided that only I could see inside my mind (I was not a Christian at this point) so I would lie until it became my truth, to try and stop people finding out who *I really was*.

Yet the lies in my life were only revealed when I realised that in private, I was masking deep despair. These two fortresses of shame and guilt had become disguised within the need to control my destiny. Certain people in my life had told me that everything was my fault. The expectations of those around me became too mighty for me to bear, and the *guilt* of feeling like I had *done something wrong* became the *shame* that I myself was *what was wrong*.

No one could find out the truth.

The fear of my reality was the only way I could protect myself and cover up who I truly was. I hid, and I hid well because the shame of being found out terrified me.

Hiding was my go-to coping mechanism to guard myself against the pain of disapproval or judgment, condemnation or mockery, belittlement or exposure, or worse; just fill in the blank of your circumstance.[66]

Inside, my heart was breaking. When I was young, I would try to seek comfort from those around me. When I became an adolescent, the comfort came from drinking alcohol and being provocative and hostile to cover up my true identity. That occurred until I believed that I was rotten to the core.

Thus the need to try and self-destruct myself intensified because, 'What do I have to lose?'

In the first chapter of this book, What Is My Purpose, I spoke about Adam and Eve in the Garden of Eden. *Guilt* and *shame* were foreign to Eden before the rebellion because creation never started out that way:

> *'So God created human beings in his own image. In the image of God he created them; male and female he created them. Then God blessed them...'.* Genesis 1:27-28

But as Eve consumed the forbidden fruit, the emotions of guilt and shame fell over her like an eclipse of the sun and moon. And as Adam followed in his wife's footsteps, two more eclipses were birthed, which meant that our inheritance was that of the same ilk.

Guilt and shame were conceived in their rebellion. The world knows guilt and shame far better than we wish, but we were never created to bear shame! Guilt is the wound from our actions, and shame is the scar we carry from the guilt. Guilt is isolated to the people themselves. Shame, unfortunately, is infectious.

When you violate God's laws, you feel guilty. But that emotion is quickly, instantaneously, joined by shame. Guilt says, 'You did something wrong'.

Shame says, 'You're pitiable. You deserve to be chastised'.

No one can share in your guilt, but many can share in your shame. The child whose father is imprisoned; the wife whose husband is unfaithful; the daughter whose mother is abusive: they all share in the shame. They feel their self-worth is lessened. Shame wraps its arms around their ankles tightly, allowing them to walk but never to run. In this way, they feel their self-worth is lessened. Shame wraps its arms around their ankles tightly, allowing them to walk but never to run. In his way, shame is far less logical than guilt.[67]

Guilt is connected to events that can be defined in objective categories that my daughter will tell you are the '5 W's': who, what, where, when, and why. But shame is far less worried about the particulars and more about the sense of feeling ashamed within and being disgraced outwardly. This was evident in the Garden of Eden when Adam and Eve hid from God:

> *'I was afraid,* [**guilt**] *because I was naked, and I hid myself* [**shame**]*'*. Genesis 3:10 ESV

The Truth of the Gospel

As soon as we become Christians, every mistake we have ever made is taken away because of Jesus Christ and what He did for us on the cross.

The guilt is taken from us; all the events that have gone wrong in our lives vanish… evaporate…gone, within a blink of an eye.

We say that heartfelt prayer when we accept Jesus as Lord and Saviour of our lives, and at that moment, we are made right with God. It is quick and conclusive, and it happens in that exchange.

But the process of applying the truth of the gospel to our lives is a lifelong battle, and it can become quite messy because shame will bother us long after we have dealt with our guilt.

God has tried to help us from the day that sin was created because while Adam and Eve are flailing around with the words of shame, hiding, fear, and blame, God goes straight to the heart of the real issue: their guilt:[68]

> *'Then the Lord God called to the man, "Where are you?" He replied, "I heard you walking in the garden, so I hid. I was afraid because I was naked." "Who told you that you were naked?" the Lord God asked. "Have you eaten from the tree whose fruit I commanded you not to eat?" The man replied, "It was the woman you gave me who gave me the fruit, and I ate it." Then the Lord God asked the woman, "What have you done?" The serpent deceived me," she replied. "That's why I ate it"'. Genesis 3:9-13*

Don't Play Games

God begins His conversation with them by addressing their wilful disobedience to His authority. 'Have you eaten from the tree that I commanded you not to eat from'? And their response? In an effort to deflect their guilt, they blame one another and the serpent.[69]

I used to play the deflecting game. I'd say anything to not have to admit to what had happened. The sense of relief when I thought that I had gotten away with something I shouldn't have!

This is mainly because there was a time when I did not understand that God is the *all-seeing, all-knowing, omniscient God*. I had not grown up in church. I had not read the Bible, and therefore I did not understand that He knew everything I did, and even my thoughts before I had even thought them. So at that point in my life, I felt that I just needed not to say anything 'out loud' and God would be none the wiser! Oh, how wrong I was:

> *'You know what I am going to say even before I say it, Lord'.* Psalm 139:4

God wants us to understand and take responsibility for our actions, but our natural response is to hide. Our shame makes us hide from God and each other, rather than running to God to deal with our guilt.[70]

It is imperative that we confront our guilt with the gospel of grace; but we must also deal with our shame by reminding ourselves of how God has dealt with our sin at the cross. He does not remember our guilt, and therefore there is nothing to be ashamed of:

> *'Farther than from a sunrise to a sunset—that's how far you've removed our guilt from us'.* Psalm 103:12 TPT

But shame will often refuse to recognise our new identity, which is why we find it so hard to let go of our past. The voice of shame will tell us that we are still our sin, but that is merely a lie.

As we turn to face Jesus and choose Him over the world, something powerful happens and those invisible shackles that have held us back from our purpose and freedom, break.

They break because we are no longer ashamed of the mistakes that we have made, or are yet to make because we understand that we can't fail God. The Holy Spirit was sent by Jesus to comfort and advise.

Therefore, when a mistake is made, we only need to run to God when the alarm bells of our consciences go off inside, to the guilt of our actions, and learn from it.

That is where we grow.

That is when shame's power is broken within our lives. No longer in prison, no longer bound because we know that the love of God conquers everything, as He endures with us through every circumstance. (1 Corinthians 13:7) We are set free from the power of sin (Romans 6:7) because Jesus took the keys of death from satan's grasp and therefore He is the one who has all authority, the keys, over death.

> *'I was dead, but now look—I am alive forever and ever. And I hold the keys that unlock death and the unseen world'.*
> Revelation 1:18 TPT

God is the One who is in control, not the enemy. Not then and indeed not today. We just need to receive that revelation.

God sees. He knows. He forgives. He redeems. And He restores, regardless of what you have done, or what has been done to you. He is calling to you to come out of hiding and into His never-ending grace: His unconditional acceptance.[71]

The Atomic Bomb

'I may not be where I want to be,
but thank God I am not where I used to be'.
Joyce Meyer

Looking back, shame was something that messed me up for many years. I remember being told during my early years as a Christian that I was going to hell because I was divorced. I naïvely believed that person.

Rather than taking that comment to God, I accepted it as truth. It became my identity. I was a divorcee who loved Jesus with everything in me, but I was not good enough. I did not make the mark.

'If only' played over in my mind for a long time. 'If only I were raised a Christian.' 'If only I had not married so young'. 'If only I had listened to my mum'. If only…if only…if only.

It was like an atomic bomb in my life that I feared had just gone off—there was no hope of survival. No coming back. Done. Gone. Dead.

I was living in fear of my shameful past, living with the disappointment of not meeting the expectation of others, the guilt of my actions, the rejection, the fear, anxiety, worry, anger, doubt… you name it, and the enemy tormented me with it. I didn't have anywhere that I thought I could turn and so, I felt alone.

Based on my track record, I assumed that someone like me had no hope of heaven, which is another one of shame's lies. Did I mention that I was messed up? I'm so glad that my mess did not deter Jesus.[72]

At 25 years old, I remember looking up into the star-filled sky, crying. I had just discovered that *I could have* been set free, but I messed it up. I now recognise that I just did not understand the fullness of God's grace at that time.

> '...he does not want any to perish but all to come to repentance'.
> 2 Peter 3:9 TPT

I was ashamed of my shame. I felt unclean. Not worthy.

When I repented of my sin and accepted Jesus into my life, I wanted it to be a blanket prayer so that I never had to deal with the individual events themselves. But that is not what we learn when we read about the woman with the issue with blood in Mark 5:24-34.

Touching Healing

This woman had been bleeding continuously for twelve years but found healing when she stepped out in courage and faith to reach Jesus and touch His cloak, who was simply walking by.

To give some context, within the culture at that time, when anyone was unclean, they were supposed to shout, 'Unclean! Unclean!' periodically to warn people around them. This was so that others would not accidentally touch them and become unclean themselves. This dates back to the laws found in the book of Leviticus, which is the Old Testament Scripture.

The Atomic Bomb

Unclean people were extremely restricted in life; they were cut off from the community.

Can you imagine the shame she felt?

To have entered into the crowd to try and reach Jesus was taking a massive risk in itself. Also, there was no way that she could have reached Jesus without touching other people, and for that she should have received the death penalty. It's no wonder that she was trembling with fear!

Perhaps the fear was because she was present in the crowds and had broken the purity laws. Maybe she was fearful of punishment. Or perhaps the trembling came from the realisation that she was free of her shame for the first time in over a decade! She was no longer captive. She was free of her past after boldly admitting to what had happened in her life when she spoke to Jesus. She found healing and we can too.

How many of us are afraid to admit that we need healing? Yet we must acknowledge *all* of our wounds. The journey from shame to freedom and full life in Christ must be a blatantly honest, nothing-hidden voyage.[73]

The Bible shows us that *we can survive* in the wild waters because we know Jesus is leading us through them. He is our Good Shepherd, whether walking beside still waters and green pastures or through the valley of the shadow of death, (Psalm 23) eventually we will step determinedly into our promised land.

When it comes to expectations, shame, guilt, or any other stronghold, we need to know that the enemy will always want to try and recapture us and take us hostage, again.

To this day, satan will periodically try to tell me that I am worthless because of my past or not good enough to achieve what God has asked me to do. Yet as hard as it is sometimes, I am determined to believe in God's truths rather than the enemy's lies.

Let's face it, this side of heaven, we are still flawed and imperfect people dealing with life in a broken, hurting world.[74] But that is why we need to defend Christian truths rather than try to distort situations and circumstances to suit our own purposes or expectations. It can only end with guilt and shame within our lives.

We need to recognise the lies and go to God in prayer. We all should be trying to become genuine disciples of Christ, and that means that we need to portray Christ in our words and behaviours faithfully.

We are all here to glorify Him, created for a purpose, with purpose.

I have learnt that when you expect the best and people do less… you are disappointed. But when you believe the best, and they do less, then you understand their story is not yet over,[75] and neither is yours!

CHAPTER NINE
JESUS' NUMBER ONE TOPIC

Money

'Money isn't the most important thing in life, but it's reasonably close to oxygen on the "gotta have it" scale'.
Zig Ziglar

Being Wise with Money

Money is one of those topics that we love to hate, hate to love, and everything else in between. It is not a coincidence that the Bible includes approximately 500 verses on both prayer and faith, but more than 2,000 on money! Money is the subject of roughly 40 percent of Jesus' parables,[76] and that is why our finances are Jesus' number one topic to speak about. This is more than heaven or hell combined, and even more than the subject of love.

Finances can change our lives in today's world, whether that be negatively or positively, and yet the Bible has a lot to say about managing money.

I feel that we can summarise this into a single word: wisdom.

We are merely to be wise with our money.

I want to talk about money from a practical standpoint quickly, but from a biblical perspective, because we need to realise a few things.

For instance:
- We are to save money, but not stash it away:
  'Don't store up treasures here on earth, where moths eat them and rust destroys them, and where thieves break in and steal'. Matthew 6:19

- We are to spend money, but with discretion and control:
  'Then he said, "Beware! Guard against every kind of greed. Life is not measured by how much you own"'. Luke 12:15

- We are to give back to the Lord, joyfully and sacrificially:
  'You must each decide in your heart how much to give. And don't give reluctantly or in response to pressure. "For God loves a person who gives cheerfully"'. 2 Corinthians 9:7

- And we are to help others, but with discernment and from the guidance of the Holy Spirit:
  'And don't forget to do good and to share with those in need. These are the sacrifices that please God'. Hebrews 13:16

The church, unfortunately, has disadvantaged themselves on the topic of money, because some individuals have taught that Christians should not be wealthy, in a worldly sense. And let's face it, there are a lot of examples of poor people in Scripture.

However, since material wealth is not an indication of God's blessing or disapproval, then we need to be careful about how we view this.

Jesus Himself did not have a home to go to, which to the world could be seen as Him being poor; but His disciples and Jesus' followers were rich in spiritual wealth if nothing else.

> 'But Jesus replied, "Foxes have dens to live in, and birds have nests, but the Son of Man has no place even to lay his head"'. Matthew 8:20

"We Just Need Faith" Is Incorrect

Following Jesus is not always easy or comfortable and most of us don't get to stay in 5-star hotels or have luxury travel within our God-given ministries, including secular roles, but it can often mean a significant cost and sacrifice to that person and their family. On the flip side of this, following Jesus might come with no earthly rewards or security.

The cost of following Jesus is high for us all, even though the outworking may look different for each of us; but the value of being Christ's disciple is even higher because that is something that lasts for eternity and has incredible rewards.

The complete opposite of being happy as a poor Christian is teaching from the 'Prosperity Gospel'. This is what individuals believe and teach as health, both physically and financially, are always the will of God for them.

We just need faith; always think positively, and we need to donate to religious causes, as it brings in a blessing from God. This isn't totally biblically correct, and apostle Paul warns Timothy about this:

> *'These people always cause trouble. Their minds are corrupt, and they have turned their backs on the truth. To them, a show of godliness is just a way to become wealthy'.* 1 Timothy 6:5

I want to show you why this isn't correct through Paul, who is seen as possibly the greatest evangelist and missionary to Gentiles, anyone who wasn't a Jew. He was used by God to do extraordinary things for His Kingdom. However, if you believe what the prosperity gospel teaches, Paul should not have suffered for Christ. His faith alone should have seen him both physically and financially blessed, and yet he suffered immensely, on more than one occasion:

> *'…I have worked harder, been put in prison more often, been whipped times without number, and faced death again and again. Five different times the Jewish leaders gave me thirty-nine lashes. Three times I was beaten with rods. Once I was stoned. Three times I was shipwrecked. Once I spent a whole night and a day adrift at sea. I have travelled on many long journeys. I have faced danger from rivers and from robbers. I have faced danger from my own people, the Jews, as well as from the Gentiles. I have faced danger in the cities, in the deserts, and on the seas. And I have faced danger from men who claim to be believers but are not. I have worked hard and long, enduring many sleepless nights. I have been hungry and thirsty and have often gone without food. I have shivered in the cold, without enough clothing to keep me warm. Then,*

besides all this, I have the daily burden of my concern for all the churches'. 2 Corinthians 11:23-28

If the prosperity gospel were the correct gospel message, then to put it simply, should Paul have endured all of those tough times?

We can learn so much from Scripture, but we need to carefully align it to what is spoken to us. What does the Word of God say about these subjects? Paul was given something, we are unsure what it was exactly, but it tormented Paul, in what he felt was to stop himself from becoming proud:

'...I was given a thorn in my flesh, a messenger from Satan to torment me and keep me from becoming proud. Three different times I begged the Lord to take it away. Each time he said, "My grace is all you need. My power works best in weakness." So now I am glad to boast about my weaknesses, so that the power of Christ can work through me. That's why I take pleasure in my weaknesses, and in the insults, hardships, persecutions, and troubles that I suffer for Christ. For when I am weak, then I am strong'. 2 Corinthians 12:7-10

Be Wise, Whether Rich or Poor

I want to show you that it's not wrong to be rich, but it is wrong to love money. It is not wrong to be poor, but it is wrong to waste money on unimportant things. The Bible's consistent message on managing money is to be wise.[77]

'Wisdom and money can get you almost anything, but only wisdom can save your life'. Ecclesiastes 7:12

This is why the Bible is full of verses about money. Jesus knew that people would desperately need wisdom when it came to their finances.

In my opinion, Jesus knew He would still be known as 'love', even though He spoke more on finances. Just because, I think, Jesus realised we would struggle with our lifestyles and spending habits more, compared to loving others.

I know many people who love others wholeheartedly, but they are either barely scraping by from living until the next wage comes in, or they are in so much debt.

Ultimately, everyone usually has some sort of an opinion about money, and that is actually really important because it reveals who we ultimately are:

> 'For your heart will always pursue what you value as your treasure'. Matthew 6:21 TPT

Desiring Money

I witnessed the desire for money. As I mentioned in a previous chapter, I was very materialistic growing up. As soon as I was old enough, I applied for all the store cards and credit cards. I wanted a big house and flashy car, so got financed for a Mercedes SLK, after all, I was 'only young once'! I wanted it all, so I tried to buy my way to happiness as that was my understanding of true happiness…money.

My dad would repeat time and time again, 'Money makes the world go around'. But I came down to reality quickly when I could no longer meet the minimum payments on the commitments I had made. My parents stepped in and bailed me out financially. I had made so many mistakes at such a young age that I thought I had learnt my lesson.

> *'But people who long to be rich fall into temptation and are trapped by many foolish and harmful desires that plunge them into ruin and destruction'.* 1 Timothy 6:9

Towards the end of 2007, unaware that the recession was about to hit the UK, Kieren and I arranged a mortgage to buy a house in England. It was an exciting time for us. We were a few weeks away from getting married and had just completed on purchasing our first marital home together. In our haste to want to get finance sorted, we didn't read the small print correctly, and it cost us dearly.

There was a large sum of money added to the mortgage by the financial advisor. By the time we had realised and contacted the relevant companies, the man had been fired because the company had discovered his actions; but we suffered dreadfully. Due to the recession, our mortgage company went into liquidation and therefore we were not able to sell as the property had gone into negative equity, which a lot of homes had. And don't even get me started on the fees to get out of the mortgage agreement! In short, we were stuck.

We could not save any money. We barely survived, living hand-to-mouth and I started working three jobs while Kieren worked all the hours God had made. All this came at a time when I became pregnant—three months after getting married.

It is true that few things have the power to throw our lives into complete chaos like a financial strain.

King Solomon was the wisest man on earth, and even he reminds us:

> *'A party gives laughter, wine gives happiness, and money gives everything'!* Ecclesiastes 10:19

Money is a subject that drives me crazy because I hate how much it controls the world. Think about it:[78]

- Money says to debt: 'I can free you'.
- Money says to vision: 'I can release you'.
- Money says to time: 'I can direct you'.
- Money says to need: 'I can help you'.

We had an out-of-control budget, which brought about anger, frustration, and pain. I hated opening mail for fear of facing another bill. Kieren and I rarely argued, but the ever-present feeling of drowning in debt meant that our relationship suffered spiritually. I blamed God at the time for not stopping this mess. Emotionally we were overwhelmed, and physically, because of the stress levels, I developed insomnia (again) and I was in and out of the hospital with various medical issues.

All of our money was spent trying to facilitate the debt that was accumulating rapidly; and with Kieren being an unbeliever at that time, the only thing we regularly argued about was my tithing to the Church needed to stop.

Kieren felt that the money was more important to be used elsewhere; and at the time, I did not understand about stewardship or what it even meant to tithe. So I stopped giving my nominal amount, and it became another element of guilt and shame that I held on to in my life.

Did you know that nearly 50 percent of couples that get divorced do so because of disagreements over money? And in addition to that, for approximately 70 percent of newlyweds, money is the issue that causes the most arguments in the first year of marriage.[79]

'Wise people know that all their money belongs to God'.
John Piper

The Epiphany Moment

I don't remember when it exactly happened, but I was trying to read the "Bible in a Year" plan on YouVersion one night. At this point, it was more like 18 months in, and still no end in sight; and I realised in my spirit that a right relationship with our finances was of great importance to God.

It was a revelation to my soul when I came across this Scripture in Luke's Gospel. I realised that God wasn't looking for the amount of money that we gave, but it was the heart behind it that ultimately mattered to Him:

> *"'I tell you the truth," Jesus said, "this poor widow has given more than all the rest of them. For they have given a tiny part of their surplus, but she, poor as she is, has given everything she has"'.* Luke 21:3-4

The ones who gave from their surplus thought nothing about it as it came more from obedience to the law. Yet the woman who gave everything did so with faith in what God would do. He was the Lord of her life; she trusted Him. It wasn't so much that she gave it all, but the money she had didn't control her.

It seemed to me from reading about different people within the Bible, those who had the most financial success were smart with their money, and also generous. They didn't just keep their money, waiting for disaster to strike, but they also gave. In other words, they had balance.[80]

> *'…You can be sure that God will take care of everything you need, his generosity exceeding even yours in the glory that pours from Jesus'*…. Philippians 4:19 MSG

I have learnt the hard way, but I now know that we cannot out-give God.

Once a fearful mess from living as a slave to money, now, although we are still not debt free (yet), there has been a massive shift in the way we look at our finances, both in the natural and supernatural.

Hence why I was so passionate about writing a chapter on money, because I remember crying with self-hatred from all of the mishandling of our finances.

Kieren and I blamed the financial advisor for many years. 'If only…' played over a lot in our conversations, but, thinking only of myself as I can't comment on Kieren's perspective, in the end it boiled down to naivety at the very least, and greed for materialistic possessions at worst. I was so excited about getting married and the idyllic future ahead of us that I didn't want to dot the i's and cross the t's.

Being bluntly honest, I wanted a house and to tell people about it at our wedding reception. I was still living the same lie that I had as a teenager, only now I was in my late twenties. It had just manifested itself in a slightly different way, but the cause was still the same, in that I cared about what people thought.

I wasn't a good steward, and it has been one of the biggest lessons in our lives.

Never again will I submit myself to the shackles of living beyond my means. Kieren and I have missed out on some pretty incredible opportunities to make things right, slowly. In doing so, it has shaped and moulded us into what God intended us to be, right from the very start.

Instead of spending everything we had, we simplified life, and it gave us some breathing room. We want to commit to living within God's provision.

Sometimes if we struggle with the power of money, then God can take us into the wilderness because it is the only way to free us from the thing that has prevented us from walking into His promised land for our lives.

For me, the financial implications we found ourselves in definitely felt like the wilderness. God needed to get us to a point at which God's power broke the power of money over our lives. His love would cleanse the shame and guilt about the financial state we were in, and the Holy Spirit could then fill us with the power to move ahead with all new financial practices.[81]

Green Pastures

It is our human nature to look for greener pastures, to wish for better circumstances, more affluence, and a more comfortable life.

We think if only I had a better job, a more beautiful house, a newer car, we would be happy. It seems logical, right? But believe me when I say, 'More money doesn't equal greater happiness'.[82]

I hope I can give you some insight over different people's stories within Luke's Gospel, a story from 2 Kings, and a parable that Jesus spoke in Matthew's Gospel. But before I do, ponder on the following question, as I think this aligns everything with where our finances are accurately:

If your true financial condition were put up on a billboard for all your friends and family to see, would you feel satisfaction and peace? Or would you feel deep embarrassment?[83]

Earlier I went through what Paul endured with his vast list of sufferings including financial issues, and yet we read in the book of Philippians:

'Not that I was ever in need, for I have learned how to be content with whatever I have. I know how to live on almost nothing or with everything. I have learned the secret of living in every situation, whether it is with a full stomach or empty, with plenty or little. For I can do everything through Christ, who gives me strength'. Philippians 4:11-13

This is beautiful. It shows us that someone who is fully joined to God, including from a financial standpoint, can accept God's current level of provision for his or her life. And even though it may go up or down throughout life, as with Paul, we can be satisfied with either scenario.

When we are anxious about things in life, especially money, it can cut back on what God wants to do through us, as we can be scared to walk by faith.

In the natural (finances, health, etc.) are things that the enemy can play on because it *does affect us*. Yet Jesus says in the following Scripture that the kingdom of God within us, the supernatural, also affects us in the natural:

> *'For the Kingdom of God is not a matter of what we eat or drink, but of living a life of goodness and peace and joy in the Holy Spirit. If you serve Christ with this attitude, you will please God, and others will approve of you, too'.* Romans 14:17-18

Who Is Lord in Your Life?

All the problems we have with money, I feel, are fundamental issues with lordship. When we allow God to reign over us, we embrace what He says, or even what He declares over our lives. We believe Him over everything else and what God thinks, rather than what we think ourselves in our limited understanding.

Let's take a few moments to consider the widow's story in 2 Kings 4:1-7.

This is a woman who has recently become widowed and is a single mum of two boys with overwhelming money problems. She seeks out Elisha in a panic because creditors are coming to take her children to be sold into slavery as they are so far behind on payments.

Essentially, Elisha tells the widow to go and collect all the jars she could from her neighbours and pour the 'small jar of olive oil', which is the only thing that she says is in her house, into what she collects. The story goes that she fills up every single jar and can then pay off all of her debts and live off what was left with her sons.

I want to look at some of the lessons that we can learn from this amazing faith-filled story:[84]

Faith doesn't make sense and will often make us uncomfortable:

Imagine being asked to gather jars from your neighbours, in faith, that God would help you. I know that I would feel awkward and maybe even embarrassed; but when the widow acted on her faith, she experienced a miracle. Sometimes faith requires us to step outside of our comfort zone so that we receive that divine blessing.

Faith is not sitting around and waiting for God to move in our lives:

Christians walk by faith, not walk once we see what we need. It requires us to get up and trust in God. Elisha could have prayed for the oil to fill the jars before the widow's very eyes, but typically, that's not God. Just like the fish and five loaves and Peter getting out of the boat, we often have to take action in our faith.

Sometimes, we haven't received because we've not asked (James 4:2):

Imagine if the widow had asked for more jars from her neighbours? She would have had even more to live off with her family! So on the flip side to that, what would have happened if the awkwardness of asking for help had got the better of her? In short, she wouldn't have had enough money to pay her debts. We need to actively reach out to others to support us, whether that is in everyday life or our ministry.

God is all about relationship with Him and others; therefore, it will never be just about you and your needs:

As mentioned, God could have just filled the jars with oil, but He often wants others to be blessed through His glory. When the neighbours helped out the widow, they would have seen God move in that miracle, which would have increased their faith as well. God cares for everyone, not just us.

We need to listen to God and not our fears:

I love that we can take this story and realise that we also can challenge ourselves to walk by faith and not by sight. God has given us a spirit of love, power, and sound mind (2 Timothy 1:7) and therefore we need to fight off the fear and step out. To move beyond the awkwardness and to boldly ask for whatever is required. To involve others, but most of all, let's challenge ourselves to listen to God because this story shows us that God will provide the oil if we'd only go out and get the jars!

God's kingdom is one of abundance; and back in the Old Testament, God told Abraham:

> '...I will bless you and make you famous, and you will be a blessing to others'. Genesis 12:2

Abraham was blessed to be a blessing because of his faithfulness to God. When God blesses us, we are to bless others also. In the Old Testament, blessings were seen in the financial provision people held.

However, in the New Testament, it is viewed differently concerning wealth and giving.

This leads me to what Jesus teaches us in the Gospels. I am going to focus on this story from Luke's Gospel:

The Rich Young Ruler (Luke 18:18-30)

This young man asks Jesus how he might obtain eternal life while pointing out that he has been faithful to keep all of the commandments from the Mosaic Law throughout his life.

Jesus responds by telling the rich young ruler to sell everything he possesses, give it to the poor, and then to follow Him. But in verse 23, Scripture tells us that the man became 'very sad.'

Unfortunately, we can read Scripture and take it in the literal sense for ourselves.

Therefore, some may question whether Jesus meant for all people to sell everything they have to follow Him. While others may ask whether Jesus meant that no rich person could ever enter into God's kingdom? I do not believe either to be correct because Jesus replies to Peter:

> *'I assure you that everyone who has given up house or wife or brothers or parents or children, for the sake of the Kingdom of God,* **will be repaid many times over in this life,** *and will have eternal life in the world to come'. Luke 18:29-30*

Nowhere in Scripture does Jesus demand this from anyone else, including other wealthy people. For example, in the very next chapter, Zacchaeus, who was the chief tax collector in the region and he had become very wealthy from it, gives half of his possessions away, and Jesus proclaims:

'Salvation has come to this home today…'. Luke 19:9

Jesus did not state to Zacchaeus, 'You only gave half away'!

I believe that Jesus gave two different answers to different people, as this is the example to us. It isn't the same for everyone because the issue has to do more with lordship rather than to the individuals themselves.

The rich young ruler had made money his idol, thus breaking the *first commandment* of the Mosaic Law, which he said he had never done:

'You must not have any other god but me'. Exodus 20:3

But he also broke the *greatest commandment* that Jesus spoke too:

'"You must love the Lord your God with all your heart, all your soul, all your strength, and all your mind." And, "Love your neighbour as yourself"'. Luke 10:27

The young ruler had shown that he loved his money more than God or anyone else for that matter. When our lordship is in money or possessions, rather than God, then there are issues with trust.

'No one can serve two masters. For you will hate one and love the other; you will be devoted to one and despise the other. You cannot serve God and be enslaved to money'. Matthew 6:24

The point Jesus was making is we cannot follow God without relinquishing our devotion to money. For the young ruler, it meant that he had to give it all away. But for Zacchaeus, giving half of his money away brought him salvation, not only into the kingdom of heaven, but salvation from the slavery of finances as well.

We should not forfeit our eternal rewards for temporary benefits.

Whom do you serve?

What can we, therefore, learn from the rich young ruler?[85]

We need to recognise Jesus as Lord.

The young man did not recognise with whom he was talking. He addresses Jesus as a 'Good Teacher', because the young ruler saw Jesus as a man of insight and depth, but he did not recognise His divine authority.

We need to be aware of our own mistakes.

Jesus was very smart with how He addressed the wealthy man. He only presented him with parts of the Mosaic Law that deal with man-to-man relationships (Luke 18:20.) All the other commandments (Exodus 20) have to do with God-to-man relationships, and this young, wealthy man had naturally not fulfilled those commands. If he had, he should have recognised Jesus as the Son of God.

Don't misunderstand God's grace.

The young ruler asked, 'What good thing must I do to have eternal life'? There is no good thing. We receive unmerited grace: the undeserved favour of a loving God, which is given freely to us—we only need to believe Jesus Christ is our Saviour and Lord. It breaks my heart that although in the natural he was wealthy, he was spiritually impoverished within his faith.

Don't walk away from Jesus.

In a way, this was the young man's only mistake because we can misunderstand all of the other points, and still be saved. If the young ruler had only committed to staying with God! The disciples' themselves did not fully understand the Lordship of Jesus, and they certainly did not fully understand the plan of grace until after the resurrection. But they stayed with Jesus, and they changed the world because they were willing to commit to learning from Him.[86]

No One Deserves Eternity

In the Gospel of Matthew, we find the Parable of the Workers Paid Equally (chapter 20). This is actually a continuation from Matthew writing about the Rich Young Man in Matthew 19:16-30, but it is important to note because this story is in response to Peter wanting to know what reward would be given to those who give up everything to follow Jesus.

Jesus, from that question, then explains the truth about the kingdom of heaven:

The owner of the vineyard went out early in the morning to hire men to work for him and agreed to pay them one denarius each as a wage. Around three hours later, the owner goes and hires more people to work in the vineyard but this time states that he will pay them 'whatever is right'. The workers seemed to trust the owner at his word, which showed his nature and character. But the owner does this again around the sixth hour, the ninth hour of the day, and lastly at the eleventh hour, just one hour before the workers finished for the day.

From verse 8, when the evening came and time for the wages to be distributed, the first group of workers saw the last group being paid one denarius, and automatically thought they would be paid more since they had worked the longest.

In verse 11 we can see that the first ones hired began to grumble against the landowner when they see they will all be paid the same, even though they received what they had agreed upon that morning.

Think about it the other way; if the owner of the vineyard had paid the ones that had worked the longest first, they would think it was fair and would have gone home without seeing the other workers get the same wage.

Yet the owner makes them watch as he pays a denarius to the ones who have only worked for an hour because our instinct is to think that we are automatically going to get more. It's as if the owner wanted to see who would become resentful of the others, or if they could actually rejoice in someone else's blessings.

Do you know that God will always make sure that we have enough?

> *'...your Father knows exactly what you need even before you ask him'!* Matthew 6:8

Therefore, we need to be careful to not feel injustice against another Christian, especially when God gives them a tremendous blessing and we get our just rewards.

Jesus can use different meanings in the parables to illustrate His point; and so if we take this parable at face value, we could ask ourselves whether we feel envious of others? Do we want the same deal that the last group of workers received rather than what we agreed upon? Do we grumble or become angry and ask, 'Why them'? Or are we able to say and mean it, 'I am happy for you'.

Yet, this story is not actually about rewards; it's about salvation. For the landowner, whose decision it was to pay all the workers the same, it was an act of mercy, not injustice, and represents God.

Grace is God's generosity, and we shouldn't begrudge others who turn to God in their last hour of life because the reality is that none of us *deserves* eternal life:

> 'For God said to Moses, "I will show mercy to anyone I choose, and I will show compassion to anyone I choose." So it is God who decides to show mercy. We can neither choose it nor work for it'. Romans 9:15-16

If we always see ourselves in need or wanting more, rather than feeling blessed with what God has promised or gives us, then we will never be able to show others the way of God's kingdom, because we will always be the ones looking for help.

We need to live within God's provision and be joyfully content whether He provides a little or a lot in any given season.[86]

This then leads me to my last point with regards to money, which is, that we need to honour God by giving Him the first tenth of ALL our earnings, for His purposes.

There is teaching on tithing in many parts of Scripture.[87] For instance, tithing can be found in the Old Testament:

> *'One-tenth of the produce of the land, whether grain from the fields or fruit from the trees, belongs to the Lord and must be set apart to him as holy'.* Leviticus 27:30

Actually, the principal of tithing began before the Mosaic Law was even introduced, through Abram:

> *'…Then Abram gave Melchizedek a tenth of all the goods he had recovered'.* Genesis 14:20

And tithing can also be found in the New Testament:

> *'What sorrow awaits you teachers of religious law and you Pharisees. Hypocrites! For you are careful to tithe even the tiniest income from your herb gardens, but you ignore the more important aspects of the law—justice, mercy, and faith.* **You should tithe, yes, but do not neglect the more important things'.** Matthew 23:23

This is something that the Church as a whole is still divided on, but the teaching on tithing can be broadly put into three categories:
1. Christians are required to tithe.
2. Christians 'should' tithe but are not technically required to do so.
3. Christians are not required to tithe.

Where you fall into those three categories is ultimately between God and you. No one can judge you but God Himself:

'They kept demanding an answer, so he stood up again and said, "All right, but let the one who has never sinned throw the first stone"'! John 8:7

From this passage, we learn that we should not accuse others unless we first thoroughly search our hearts and minds to make sure that we are pure in every possible aspect.

'And why worry about a speck in your friend's eye when you have a log in your own'? Matthew 7:3

However, I believe, we should tithe, because throughout this chapter, we have seen the power that money has over us, and returning the first tenth to God determines and makes a statement about who has the authority over our lives. It is always our own choice, but one the Bible treats as divinely important.[88]

Faithfulness Over Burdens

One of the life-changing experiences I had was when I went to Vanuatu in 2014 on a mission trip. During one of the outreaches, I spoke to one of the families in Port Vila. Compared to Western viewpoints, they had very little in regards to wealth and possessions.

Homes were generally galvanised steel with dirt floors, no windows, running water, or electricity, and one room where the whole family ate, slept, and communed. But it was as if the lady could read my mind as she simply said, "We pray for you. You look at us and see little, but we look at you and feel sorry that you have so many burdens over material things. You have too much choice."

The people of Port Vila were among the happiest people I have ever come across because they lived simple lives full of love and faith for God, as they knew that He was their ultimate Provider and He alone sustained them (their words). It didn't matter what they had, they felt blessed regardless of their circumstances; and yet, I watched them still give to the church. I learnt a lot from them with regards to being faithful.

When the Bible asks us to take the first tenth of all of our earnings and give it to God's storehouse, it requires faith, because it means we are committing to living beneath the full provision we have received from God.

In the passage in Malachi, it is the only time found in the Bible that God says we can test Him. And this is with regards to our finances. Test Him to see that He will provide if we give what was His in the first place.

Test Him to see if heaven won't pour out a blessing when we submit to His sovereignty:

> '"Bring all the tithes into the storehouse so there will be enough food in my Temple. If you do," says the Lord of Heaven's Armies, "I will open the windows of heaven for you. I will pour out a blessing so great you won't have enough room to take it in! Try it! Put me to the test"'! Malachi 3:10

A to B or A to C

I always loved the analogy found in the book *Simplify* by Bill Hybels. Bill talks about when we live on 100 percent of what God gives us, it gets us from A to B.

When we listen to what the Word of God says, we not only get from A to B on just 90 percent of our earnings but as a reward of our faith and obedience, God will not only take us to A to B but from B to C as well. The B to C living is where God pours out His blessings, as mentioned in Malachi.

We never are going to know what C will look like until we step out in faith. Since Kieren and I applied this concept to our lives, we have had many C stories.

Kieren will always tell you that he struggled with letting go of finances, but it even became a problem with gambling when he thought that a 'big win' would be the answer to solving our life's issues.

I talked about this principle from the Scripture. It wasn't until Kieren said he would 'give God three months' to prove me wrong, that we began tithing 10 percent, and have been ever since, because God showed up.

We have stories of answered prayer, favour, protection, new friendships, new opportunities, and unexpected blessings that have come our way.

There is nothing quite like living in obedience from A to B and knowing that God has a C story in mind for you as well![89]

> *'Most people fail to realise*
> *that money is both a test and trust from God'.*
> *Rick Warren*

CHAPTER TEN

YES, WE SHOULD LOVE SEX

Let's Get Straight to the Point

'Sex is a bit like glue. You shouldn't apply it until you're absolutely sure you're ready to stick two things together permanently'.
Andy Stanley

This is the chapter that everyone generally wants to read. After all, the title should spark our interest, if nothing else!

It's human instinct, our very nature to be intrigued by life, to desire, to dream, and to actually love sex with our husband or wife. We were designed and formed with sex in mind; and ultimately, it was God's idea for intimacy. It was His idea for sex, and it was definitely His idea for orgasms; so who says God isn't good?

Sex is a beautiful thing. The very notion of being able to give yourself to the exact person you were destined to be with when God wrote your story in His Book: just to give yourself to your spouse without fear or condemnation, no shame or wondering, freely and wholeheartedly; is compelling and deep-seated in thinking, but it is actually the very essence of what God intended for us all.

Yes, *we should love sex*, but we should love it in the way that God intended. God could have created us to reproduce the way plants do, with floating pollen—now there's a thought! But, He preferred human life to be birthed from the blissful and loving embrace of intercourse.

It makes sense that the All-Knowing God, who invented sex, should know how it could best be celebrated. And yet people still naturally think that the equation for God is: God + Sex = Boredom.

In all honesty, I thought the same. Remember, I was not born and raised as a Christian girl. I watched a cartoon growing up where the devil was on one shoulder and the angel was on the other side, in Tweety and Sylvester, and I always thought that the devil seemed to have more fun.

I lived in a world of obsession, watching pornographic videos from a ridiculously young age. My teenage years saw the world open up even more with the arrival of the Internet. It instantly became possible for me to look at everything I ever wanted, 24 hours per day.

The things that I saw gave me the impression that women either became 'powerful' with regards to sex—bargaining and even demanding to get what they wanted in return for sex. Or women were treated like objects. I also developed a warped sense of what true beauty was due to watching porn and reading all the magazine articles on 'how to keep your man'. I even spoke about this in the earlier chapter titled, Broken but Healed; I spent so much money on trying to perfect myself, that I forgot what real beauty was.

I had a need and a desire to look a certain way. No longer was I going to be shy and reserved. I felt 'alive' when I got attention; all eyes were on me, and I thought that was what I wanted. I thought my sexuality was a tool to find true love, hopefully.

My dad would remind my brother and me that if he ever had his time again, he wouldn't have gotten married and definitely wouldn't have had children. 'We shouldn't want to get tied down', Dad would say, and we were to 'Go and have fun, as the world is our oyster'!

My peers sought to have the freedom to do what they wanted with their bodies. People would boast about the number of partners they had had so far, and there was a hunger to go and 'get laid' over the lunchtimes at school, let alone when we could get into the nightclubs from our mid-teens onwards.

It was generally deemed normal to have sex before a relationship even began. Therefore, it became like a never-ending story of one-night stands and people being passed around, like the spinning wheel game.

People would cheer on friends who were about to embark in casual sex with the same person they had conquered, giving them tips or warnings of what to expect. Everyone numb to the random hook-ups that took place and the contrariness of it all.

I thank God that this was something that I didn't embark in, and although I wish that I could forget some of the choices that I made before finding Christ, it has shaped me into who I am today. This passage speaks volumes in the way life was for me:

> *'It is obvious what kind of life develops out of trying to get your own way all the time: repetitive, loveless, cheap sex; a stinking accumulation of mental and emotional garbage; frenzied and joyless grabs for happiness; trinket gods; magic-show religion; paranoid loneliness; cutthroat competition; all-consuming-yet-never-satisfied wants; a brutal temper; an impotence to love or be loved; divided homes and divided lives; smallminded and lopsided pursuits; the vicious habit of depersonalising everyone into a rival; uncontrolled and uncontrollable addictions; ugly parodies of community. I could go on...'.*
> Galatians 5:19-21 MSG

It's about time that we talked about sex and all that it brings. We need to stop shying away from this topic because, in truth, we all need to be open and honest with ourselves. I don't mean that we need to be shouting from the rooftops about our struggles or accomplishments, but in all seriousness, sex has been so twisted from its original purpose that we now look to sex as something we obsess over. We lust after it, and that is not a good thing.

Society has created so many myths around sex that we have become consumers in the enemy's twisted and perverse take on what was initially God-given.

When God pressed on my heart to write this book, I knew that one of the chapters was going to be on sex. My testimony up until finding God was the harsh reality of living for the world. But God has since redeemed and restored me, some things or events I have endured are a testimony of decidedly bad decisions. Yet God is able to still work them together for good. I still don't have it all together, but I know by God's grace I can take one day at a time, especially in the way that I think about myself:

> *'So we are convinced that every detail of our lives is continually woven together to fit into God's perfect plan of bringing good into our lives, for we are his lovers who have been called to fulfil his designed purpose'.* Romans 8:28 TPT

I have made *many* mistakes, but God saw the bigger picture before I even gave my life to Him, and His master plan ensures that I am ultimately made into whom He created me to be, as long as I remain focused on Him.

This is why I feel I have the ability to speak into this topic. I pray that my openness will be used for God's exaltation, because if I can make one person think differently about what the real effects regarding sex are, then maybe his or her testimony won't be one that is shattered, but more that the person had the strength to walk a different path.

Sex Outside of Marriage

So I want to throw some things out there for us to ponder over. For instance, we might have a viewpoint that we can give ourselves to another person, and there is no fear or shame in our life from that. But by the end of this chapter I hope to show that although the implications of casual sex might not be shining through in our lives right now, our moral compass—our underlying belief system in how we view others and ourselves—might be slowly bubbling under the surface and we haven't even given it a thought.

'Run from anything that stimulates youthful lusts. Instead, pursue righteous living, faithfulness, love, and peace. Enjoy the companionship of those who call on the Lord with pure hearts'.
2 Timothy 2:22

I am tired of the acceptance of our 'try before you buy' attitude. We live in an era when we have been desensitised; and because of this controversial topic, we are afraid to speak up.

It doesn't help that most of the Church seems afraid to talk about it either, which is leaving a lot of people exposed, obsessed, and warped in thinking with regards to the effects of sex, and the power that it has over us.

It is interesting to note though, that the change of modern urban lifestyles around the world—including more years of schooling, career development, independent living, tolerance of diversity and greater degree of anonymity—have contributed to the rise in premarital sex. Yet, in developing countries, in contrast, large majorities still continue to consider premarital sex morally unacceptable.[90]

Statistics show within the United States alone (2016) that a staggering 67 percent feel that sex before marriage is morally acceptable and divorce now has an acceptance rate of 71 percent among the American population.[91] Yet in another survey, 70.6 percent of Americans stand as Christians.[93]

This is why we need to speak up. These figures in the USA alone show why our thinking needs to change and the global statistics are just as disconcerting. As Christians, God calls us to a higher standard because He calls us to be like Christ and to put Him first in our lives. The Bible says:

> *'Don't copy the behaviour and customs of this world, but let God transform you into a new person by changing the way you think. Then you will learn to know God's will for you, which is good and pleasing and perfect'. Romans 12:2*

You haven't done more, or experienced worse, compared to the next person. And being honest, I'm in the same boat as most, because I have had my fair share of struggles too, some of which I have talked to you about; but I hope that in writing this book you receive revelation from God that you are loved, and you are understood.[94]

There is an on-going battle within society because sex was meant to be an awesome experience between husband and wife to provide physical, emotional, and spiritual intimacy in love, as well as being fulfilled by each other. Yet sadly, the world does not operate like that any longer, and those statistics confirm this.

Our bodies have been stolen from us, and we don't even realise it. We have this mindset that we can use them to do whatever we like, and there are no consequences. No penalties to our emotional and spiritual well-being when we watch *that movie*, or listen to *those songs*, or look at *porn*, whether on a DVD, YouTube, mobile devices, or magazines. All of them have the ability to shape and mould us, with overwhelming negative results. I know because I have lived it, I have seen the devastation firsthand.

If we rise up to educate people without fear of persecution, then it can only lead to revelation, and revelation will lead to transformation—but only when we accept God's definition as truth.[95]

We need to understand or have the capacity to appreciate the correct meaning of sex in God's design. Because then we generally know the why behind the what. We begin to understand that what *we want* and what *we need*, are two different things. Therefore, we need to look beyond the apparent goals in life to discover what we really want.

Sadly, we live in a warped but shared mindset, which teaches us that we 'must have it now', as then we're happy. If we are wealthy, good-looking, successful, and having wild, carefree sex, then we must be *really* happy. That isn't what I feel we really want though; as it's more to do with what we believe those things will bring us.

When we cut through all the gobbledygook of life, ultimately we all have the same basic desires and needs: fulfilment, happiness, peace, love, acceptance, respect, and connection…sound familiar?

> *'But the Holy Spirit produces this kind of fruit in our lives: love, joy, peace, patience, kindness, goodness, faithfulness, gentleness, and self-control…'.* Galatians 5:22-23

Nobody needs a one-night stand or a quick meaningless fling, but we all need love. Nobody should need to be seen as equal; we all need connection, acceptance, and understanding. Nobody needs to be seen as promiscuous and carefree; we all need peace and happiness. The problem is, we live in a culture that teaches that one equals the other.

If only society taught that real happiness is far more about what's happening in our internal nature than our external one because it's a commonly held belief that we're all very different and we all have different goals. But in many ways, we're not, and we don't; we all want essentially the same things, it's just the enemy has taken our attention off what really matters:[96]

> 'The thief's purpose is to steal and kill and destroy...'. John 10:10

First and foremost we must understand that satan's primary target is in the lives of humanity. Therefore, I want to give you some context so that you understand what satan is trying to do.

We are called a 'triune being' made up of a spirit, soul, and body. This means that our spirit and soul are different but inseparable, and are housed in a physical body:

> '...may your whole spirit and soul and body be kept blameless until our Lord Jesus Christ comes again'. 1 Thessalonians 5:23

The evil one's *primary target is the soul* of humankind. Which is made up of our mind, will, and emotions. This is our self-conscious part, it knows who we are. But our soul and body are the results of natural reproduction, which means that our nature and characteristics have traits from our parents—these, unfortunately, go against God and have been passed down through generation to generation.[97]

> 'For I was born a sinner—yes, from the moment my mother conceived me'. Psalm 51:5

If satan can get our soul reprogrammed to think, act, and feel the way he wants us to, then he has control of what goes on in areas of our lives.

The primary thing the enemy wants to *steal* from us, *put to death* in our lives, and utterly *destroy,* is our faith in God. If satan can get us to think and believe things that are contrary to the Word of God, he can begin to get into our belief systems.

Therefore, we need to look to the Word of God because He gives us clear guidance on how we can best experience the gift of intimacy and love through sex. God is the only One who can answer this because there are everlasting repercussions at stake. He never intended for sex to be used the way that it currently is.

One myth that satan wants us to live by is that sex is only physical.

Sex Is Only Physical[98]

I know this is a shocking revelation, but we live in a society that thinks as long as nobody gets pregnant, gets a disease, or gets hurt, then 'Wham bam thank you ma'am or sir'.

Yet, that is so far from the truth! I think deep down we already know this, because if we treat sex as just an act between two mutual, consenting people, ultimately we hurt ourselves. But eventually, when people get married, they hurt their spouse as well. For us who are already married, we are dealing with the effects of bad sexual choices; and sadly, we don't even understand what the association is.

I was in this category of thinking. I wish someone had taken the time to explain things to me with regards to sex, to make me understand what my real worth was. Because it *does matter!* We were created with a greater purpose. We should feel that our body is more precious than gold, rubies, or whatever you see as the most precious item in the world, as you were created in the image of the Most High:

> *'Then God said, "Let us make human beings in our image, to be like us…"'. Genesis 1:26*

We were made to be a one of a kind. We were made in a way that science still can't quite comprehend. So why do we treat our bodies so carelessly?

> *'You made all the delicate, inner parts of my body and knit me together in my mother's womb. Thank you for making me so wonderfully complex! Your workmanship is marvellous…'.* Psalm 139:13-14

Why do we teach primary age children about the process of sexual intercourse and fundamentally forget about the most complex system in the body concerning the supreme sexual organ: our brain? This is where billions of neurons are shaping us into the humans we are, and the act of sex is no different to how we think or feel.

Sex cannot only be surface level and physical! We are emotional and spiritual beings. Therefore, we are God's ultimate creation with immeasurable worth, value, beauty, and purpose. We do not need a partner to tell us our value to them, because our true identity is found in Christ.[99]

Our behaviours are important and carry more tenacity than we acknowledge, as there are more implications to our sexual expression than we comprehend. Our sexual conduct is on a much deeper level, for if it was just physical, then every one of us could shake off the emotions we face and move on with our lives after each partner we had. No questions asked, no need for relationship, just raw, physical, happy sex.

Let's cut to the chase; if sex was just physical, then why is rape more devastating to a person than merely just being beaten up? Why do more people report about being beaten up but then carry the action of the rape with them throughout their lives because they feel they can't tell anyone?

Statistics show that men and women do not report a startling 63 percent of sexual assaults.[100] I never reported the abuse I endured, so I know the feeling of the shame I felt. Yet even now, I can still be triggered by an innocent action. It's that sense of helplessness that floods my body, and I instantly become gripped with emotion until I can rationalise my surroundings.

Although only a millisecond for me, for some people those feelings can last a lifetime because they need to work through their emotions; and unfortunately, they might believe that they will never be able to overcome them.

> *'Sex is a momentary itch; Love never lets you go'.*
> **Kingsley Amis**

Sex Is More than a Bit of Fun

Another myth that satan loves to use is that *sex is only a bit of fun*. Now I am not going to say that isn't fun, as it is, and the Bible has so many Scriptures regarding that, but satan tends to leave out one of the fundamental parts.

Remember that satan loves to twist the truth in what the Word of God says. For example, I was struck recently at how well satan knows the Bible and how he loves to quote Scripture to destroy faith. Go back to the book of Matthew and see how he tried to persuade Jesus to throw Himself down from the Temple roof. He argued *from Scripture:*

> *'If you are the Son of God, jump off! For the Scriptures say, "He will order his angels to protect you..."'*. Matthew 4:6

Interestingly, satan does not always try to ruin our faith by saying, 'The Bible isn't true'. He often seeks to destroy our faith by twisting the truth on some passage and using it to lead us into rebellion.

The temptation to go have a bit of fun is never followed by the reality of what indeed occurs when we embark on casual sex outside of marriage.

When Moses went up the mountain to get the Ten Commandments, every pagan culture celebrated sex and religion. There was no such thing as marital fidelity, so the cultures of that time would have laughed at such an idea.

Therefore, if you were Moses up on a mountain with God, and you had the opportunity to fool all of these people waiting for you (because they all think that you are a prophet) yet, you knew that this Christianity lark was all a sham, what would you have written about sex?

Yes, We Should Love Sex

In every single cult that we are familiar with, some guy has always twisted the rules that allows him and others to have sex with multiple women.

Yet Moses came down from that mountain and stated that our relationships should be one man and one woman for life:

> 'You must not commit adultery'. Exodus 20:14

Then Jesus echoed it:

> 'Since they are no longer two but one, let no one split apart what God has joined together'. Matthew 19:6

And then the apostle Paul goes into the city of Corinth and brings an instruction that was not religious; because as I mentioned, all of the other religions thought that sex outside of marriage was ok, and says:

> 'Run from sexual sin'! 1 Corinthians 6:18

He goes on to define sexual sin as sex outside of marriage:

> 'But because there is so much sexual immorality, each man should have his own wife, and each woman should have her own husband'. 1 Corinthians 7:2

But, if we go back to the previous Scripture, Paul says:

> '...No other sin so clearly affects the body as this one does. For sexual immorality is a sin against your own body'. 1 Corinthians 6:18

In other words, every kind of sin that people commit is like no other because sin is generally committed outside of our own bodies. But those who sin sexually, which Paul describes as sex outside of marriage, is sinning against their own bodies.

Paul is merely saying that when you sin sexually, you hurt yourself. And not only do you hurt yourself, but you do it at the deepest level.

Paul uses a word that shocks his audience a few chapters before. He says:

> *'And don't you realise that if a man joins himself to a prostitute, he becomes one body with her? For the Scriptures say, "The two are **united** into one"'*. 1 Corinthians 6:16

They would have looked at the word *united* flabbergasted because the Greek word would have made no sense to them. They would have said that they weren't 'uniting' with the prostitutes, they were just having sex; but the Greek word Paul uses means 'like glue… can't be separated'.

Paul was saying that when you have sex with a person, there is a sense of permanence. You become one with that person. Paul was saying that it's not just physical; it's as personal as anything imaginable because God designed it that way. You were intended to become one with one person.

And when you continue to become one with person after person after person, you damage your intimacy factor. You hurt your ability to experience what God created and intended you to experience, you disconnect, and over time you become numb. This is where your meant-to-be, God-given relationship suffers.

Then Paul goes back to the book of Genesis to prove his point:

> '...*the two are united into one*'. Genesis 2:24

That is the intimacy word *united*, because it's about two individuals becoming one, and that one can't be *un-oned*.

In 1 Corinthians it says:

> 'God bought you with a high price. So you must honor God with your body'.
> 1 Corinthians 6:20

In other words, your body is not your body. If you are a Christian, then all of you belongs to God because you have been bought at a price, purchased and redeemed through Jesus. Christ paid the full amount to set us free. (Galatians 3:13 TPT) Therefore Paul says, *honour God with your bodies*.

Sex Within Marriage

A scenario that I hear about often is people in sexless marriages or couples who struggle with sex within marriage itself. Why is it for some of us, we feel dead from the waist down and have no desire to be with our husband or wife, especially as I just said God only wants us to be with our spouse?

Only to then find you have an attractive work colleague, for example, who just so happens to *now* catch your eye when things are rough at home. I mean, who wants to be in a sexless relationship anyway, it's obviously a sign! Plus, the grass is always greener on the other side, when you live in the desert:

> *'But I say, anyone who even looks at a woman with lust has already committed adultery with her in his heart'.* Matthew 5:28

As mentioned previously, the devil is looking for ways for you to think outside of what the Bible talks about. So if we have a marriage where one person is struggling with sex or one partner who has a higher sex drive than the other, then the enemy is going to look for ways to tempt us.

> *'Do not deprive each other of sexual relations, unless you both agree to refrain from sexual intimacy for a limited time so you can give yourselves more completely to prayer. Afterward, you should come together again so that Satan won't be able to tempt you because of your lack of self-control'.* 1 Corinthians 7:5

We are not supposed to be in a marriage where we purposefully take away sex to make our partner 'pay' or to 'get back at them'. This Scripture is clear that it is only when both parties agree to refrain from sex that it should happen, but only for a limited time because then satan can't tempt us.

Most problems within marriage can be due to a lack of communication, but lovers can be reconciled, commitment can be renewed, and romance can be refreshed towards each other. When we allow the enemy into our marriage, into our beds, the walls of deception cover our eyes, so we need to be careful that we take care of problems while they are still small.

Other than that, sex should be enjoyable! If an activity you're doing doesn't bring enjoyment to both partners, it will cause resentment and distance between you. That's not part of our design. God created us to become one:

> *'Therefore a man leaves his father and mother and embraces his wife. They become one flesh'.* Genesis 2:24 MSG

When God gave us direction for sex, He did so to either protect us from harm or to provide for our needs, or both. That is why the Bible is very honest about sex. God's not a prude. Just read the Song of Solomon; the whole book celebrates the erotic love of a husband and wife. We see their relationship unfold, and the intense power that love has affects their hearts, their minds, and their bodies. Sex in an intimate way is an integral part of our identities; and therefore, sex isn't merely recreational or consensual, it is an act of worship through which two human beings reflect the image of God. The God who is more than one Person and yet One.[102]

Song of Solomon shows us why we need marriage. It's to self-guard our love for one another. Marriage merely is love that is celebrated, and it also demonstrates a commitment to each other.

Sex Outside Marriage Is Not Intimacy

The thing that makes sex on a much deeper level is because God gave sex to us as an expression of intimacy with Him. Yes, that's right. God gave us sex so that we would be intimate with Him. In other words, to know and to be fully known.

A married couple in a long-term, committed relationship enters into a more secure and trusting ground with each additional sexual encounter they have. Therefore, sex can then indeed become about 'making love' rather than just 'having sex'. This is why having multiple partners creates doubt and performance comparisons, as they are barriers to the deepest levels of intimacy.

Kieren and I went through periods within our marriage when sex brought doubt, and therefore we struggled. Not that we doubted our marriage, but both of us had had previous partners and combining that with my many health issues at the time, it would see us go for long periods of not being able to be intimate.

The problem we then faced was that we would second-guess ourselves that the other didn't want sex. We thought that the other person was too tired or too stressed, etc. and this caused barriers in our actual relationship itself because our intimacy suffered. When I look back, the enemy would play on the fact we had been intimate with other people, and thus the question came about, 'What is wrong with me'?

The Bottom Line (no pun intended)

God created sex; He gave it to dogs, horses, and even flies. But then He created us and took sex to a whole new level.

It was no longer just procreation; God created something that we would experience together, and He intended for us to experience that same type of intimacy with Him.

Sex is the ultimate expression of understanding because just as God knows us intimately, He gives us the same invitation to know Him more by developing our relationship.

Encounters with the living King are intended to deepen our love. We are to want more of Him, just as God wants all of us. This was God's design for marriage as well, to let your husband or wife know you like no else has, and that's why we should love sex!

That's the bottom line when it comes to following Jesus' words on sex. It's a question of whether we believe our lives, sexual or otherwise, belong to Him, or to ourselves.

If we want to live for Jesus, then He tells us that sex is even better than we thought. Not only can we enjoy it far better within its proper, God-created context, but we are also reflecting the glory of the Trinity when we do! It also means that Jesus wants to be Lord of what we do because our whole lives belong to Him.

Jesus is clear that sex is reserved for lifelong marriage between one man and one woman, and that He created it to be incredibly fun so that we would make love often and enjoy it.

If you are not living this way, then sex should not be a reason for you to reject Jesus but for you to accept Him. Our culture is full of good ideas for bad sex, but Jesus promises that if we follow the Maker's instructions, then sex gets better. He also promises you forgiveness as He did the adulterous woman:

> *'I certainly don't condemn you...Go, and from now on, be free from a life of sin'.* John 8:11 TPT

If you are not yet married but are trying to live Jesus' way, then you should be encouraged. God will bless your decision to remain celibate until you marry. It's not a sin to remain single, even for your entire life, and only a select few have that calling on their life, the apostle Paul being one of them.

Singleness is also not a curse; there is nothing wrong with you, and you are not a 'second-class Christian'. The most important thing to remember in life is that it's not about finding a mate and having children, but serving God:

> *'You are blessed because you believed that the Lord would do what he said'*. Luke 1:45

And if you are married, Jesus' encourages you to go and make love to your husband or wife because *we should love sex!*[103]

> **'I didn't marry The One, I married this one,
> and the two of us became one'.
> Matt Walsh**

CHAPTER ELEVEN

RISE AND SHINE

Life has Battles, but Jesus has the Victory!
It's Time to Rise and Fight!

'What's coming against me is only training for where God is taking me'.
Steven Furtick

Fairy Tales of Faith

When I first became a Christian, I would love to look for all the self-help books—Christian or non-Christian. From this, I developed a warped image of God, and in my head, He became like my fairy godmother.

I wanted God to wave His magic wand and poof, all of my problems would magically disappear because so many times I heard it was just about having faith. And I knew that I had enough faith for my miracles!

After all, that's what the Bible says, right?

I would read the following Scripture and then talk to God about my wants and desires. I assumed He created me to be happy; and therefore to me, happy wasn't how I was living at the time. So I told God His to-do list for my life:

> *'"You don't have enough faith," Jesus told them. "I tell you the truth, if you had faith even as small as a mustard seed, you could say to this mountain, 'Move from here to there,' and it would move. Nothing would be impossible"'.* Matthew 17:20

The reality of life is so much more than fairy tales, and I came down with a bump after the giddiness of finding Christ. Yes, I had miraculous healings and abundant blessings that could only have come from the Lord; but for the best part, the daily grind I faced became more like a battlefield. I lost, badly, time and time again.

So, I want to briefly tell you what I have found, as I feel that this is a reality for a lot of believers within the church today, and even for those who have unfortunately walked away from God.

I did not understand what it truly meant to be on this journey with Christ; and at some stages in my journey, honestly, a part of me thought, *What's the point?* I still had all of the pain and suffering that I previously felt. God wasn't following through with His promises; otherwise, surely I would have been happy?

In truth, I had not been taught about studying the Bible, or that having a relationship with God is two-way communication. My faith was based on talking to Him about my wants and needs. That meant I would find Scripture to show that God had done that thing I needed before, because if He had, then God would *have to* do it again for me. Yet, when that didn't happen, the offence would build towards God. *I felt like I was being rejected all over again,* and I got caught up in doubting who God was because I assumed He was something He's not.

I had created a god that didn't exist; and just like we see from any other cult, those other gods will always let us down because Yahweh, our God, is the one and only true God. (Deuteronomy 6:4 MSG)

I realise now that I needed to realign my fact-based desires with God's truth. When I received faith-filled answers from Him, it didn't make sense to me because I was still a baby in my faith; and being brutally honest, I think many of us still are today:

> *'…As long as you grab for what makes you feel good or makes you look important, are you really much different than a babe at the breast, content only when everything's going your way?'*
> 1 Corinthians 3:3 MSG

How many of us still do not understand our purpose for being alive, let alone what it means to be growing in our faith?

We question our very existence. Doubt the reason for our need to breathe.

We feel alone. Or we are just fed up with life because of the hopelessness. If that is the case for you, then like myself, I felt like a merry-go-round of pointlessness because my faith kept going around and around in circles since I had the same struggles, fears, and longings as the next person.

Andy Stanley covers this well, and the following types of gods are adapted from one of his podcasts.[104] Andy discusses that the gods we create, ultimately mean we lose faith in who God really is.

This isn't something to get embarrassed about; humanity, after all, has been doing this since the beginning of time. For instance, there was a period in which people believed in worshipping the sun. Now thankfully most people have since stopped this, but we have then moved on and found another god:

> 'We are all atheists about most of the gods that humanity has ever believed in. Some of us just go one god further'.
> Richard Dawkins

The reality is, for some of us we struggle with the God we have heard about, or even read about, compared to the realisation of Him in our lives.

We fight with the adult answers towards our childlike faith only because it doesn't match our expectations of Him. Our foundations have been built incorrectly, and so when a tremor occurs in our lives, devastation hits, and we then walk away from God.

> 'Anyone who listens to my teaching and follows it is wise, like a person who builds a house on solid rock. Though the rain comes in torrents and the floodwaters rise and the winds beat against that house, it won't collapse because it is built on bedrock. But anyone who hears my teaching and doesn't obey it is foolish, like a person who builds a house on sand. When the rains and floods come and the winds beat against that house, it will collapse with a mighty crash'. Matthew 7:24-27

The following are 'types of gods' that we can believe in. Unfortunately, these are usually from somebody telling us that this is who God is and then we have accepted it as truth, to then believe it as well.

Do any of these sound familiar to you?

Bodyguard God

> *"Bad things never happen to good people."* This statement is not biblical because Jesus was a very good Person who died horrifically, as did most of the Christians in the first century. Therefore, if this was who God was, then Christianity would never have made it past that time in history. The following Scripture shows us that *we will go through adversity,* but God is good because He will help us get through those times of need in this inherently bad world:
>
> *'...When you walk through the fire of oppression, you will not be burned up; the flames will not consume you'.* Isaiah 43:2

On-Demand God

This was who I believed God was: *I demand and God should provide.* We believe God needs to answer our prayers when we pray for them, and unfortunately, this doesn't generally happen! No sign. No miracles. Therefore God can't be real.

Why do we believe that God will respond to what we expect, want, or need? The truth is that life is not about us. It's not about what we want, but that we would fulfil all that God created us to be.

When we pray for the things that God wants, it will be done. And I thank God now that He never answered certain prayers of mine, because He really does know best:

> 'We can make our plans, but the Lord determines our steps'. Proverbs 16:9

Imaginary God

This is when we assume that if we can feel God's presence, then obviously, He is with us. Yet, we want to sense Him all the time; and therefore when we don't, we rationalise that God's not really there. We need to remember that we are least aware of the things that become most constant or familiar in our lives. Which makes sense, because God is walking with us every step of every single day:

> '…Yet I am not alone because the Father is with me'. John 16:32

Guilt/Shame God

This is the god that we feel always tells us *"No."* Therefore, when we do things, he makes us feel guilty. This is the god that you feel doesn't like you because all you hear is the same thing. But, although we may have walked away from this god, the guilt and shame remain in our lives. The truth is that God does love us, and He has an amazing future planned for us, but as we learnt in a previous chapter, shame does not come from God:

> '"For I know the plans I have for you," says the Lord. "They are plans for good and not for disaster, to give you a future and a hope"'. Jeremiah 29:11

Anti-Science God

This is when we believe that we have to choose between undeniable sciences compared to an unreliable religion. This is when we are taught the subject in school and can see what is in front of us, but we feel we need to pick. This is when we don't want to believe that 'we have to stop thinking, just to believe in God'. The truth is that science helps us in knowledge and understanding of God, to apply His rules for creation for His glory. In other words, science reveals God's creation to us. Solomon asked for wisdom, and God gave Him an incredible ability to talk about creation with authority:

> *'He could speak with authority about all kinds of plants, from the great cedar of Lebanon to the tiny hyssop that grows from cracks in a wall. He could also speak about animals, birds, small creatures, and fish'.* 1 Kings 4:33

Gap God

This is the god that is the reason for everything that we can't explain. Yet this undermines our faith because what is unexplainable today might be explainable tomorrow. For instance, as science develops, we would like to think that we could find a permanent cure for cancer, but if our faith is based on Him being all of the unexplainable things, when the world explains whatever it is, faith is destroyed. Unexplainable is more about our lack of understanding in that situation. Our mind will generally fill in the blank with what makes sense to us, but God is not the reason for everything we can't comprehend. It is ok for Christians not to know everything, but it is dangerous for us to use God to bridge the gap and make Him the reason when we lack understanding:

> *'For everything there is a season, a time for every activity under heaven'.*
>
> Ecclesiastes 3:1

The gods mentioned do not exist, so if you have believed in one of them, you're right; they're not real. But that doesn't mean that the God Most High (Psalm 57:2 El Elyon) isn't real.

Our viewpoint should not be the defining reality of who God is. We merely had the wrong god that we looked to within our lives, and therefore it's more about us realigning to whom God actually is. He is Sovereign, He is Unchanging, and He is the Eternal God who is and who was and who is to come, the Almighty! (Revelation 1:8 NIV)

If these types of gods are the lies that you have believed and they stopped you from receiving all of God's love or even made you walk away, then I encourage you to ask for forgiveness from God. Psalm 51 is a beautiful prayer from David; the following is a small sample of what he said to come back to God:

> *'Let my passion for life be restored, tasting joy in every breakthrough you bring to me. Hold me close to you with a willing spirit that obeys whatever you say. Then I can show to other guilty ones how loving and merciful you are. They will find their way back home to you, knowing that you will forgive them. O God, my saving God, deliver me fully from every sin, even the sin that brought bloodguilt. Then my heart will once again be thrilled to sing the passionate songs of joy and deliverance! Lord God, unlock my heart, unlock my lips, and I will overcome with my joyous praise'!* Psalm 51:12-15 TPT

So, how do we win *Life's Greatest Battles?*

There are two fundamentals ways that I believe are God's will for every one of us and what allows us to walk in true freedom. This is because these things I write about give us the *why* behind the *what*.

The first one I will talk about now; and the final way is discussed in the last chapter.

So what is the first fundamental to start winning the battles we face?

Choose Joy

> *'Always be joyful. Never stop praying. Be thankful in all circumstances, for this is God's will for you who belong to Christ Jesus'.* 1 Thessalonians 5:16-18

Cliché? Nope, fortunately not!

I spoke about the mind in the previous chapter titled, Yes, We Should Love Sex, and how satan's number one goal is to get us to think differently about what God's Word says, because then he will win the battles we face.

However, when we change the way we think, in turn, that will change the way we feel, because even though you and I may believe in Christ, we can certainly still think according to this world:

> *'The mind governed by the flesh is death, but the mind governed by the Spirit is life and peace'.* Romans 8:6 NIV

When we do not make the deliberate choice to think according to the Spirit, we tend to default to what the world or flesh says. You might not be able to control the way you feel, but you can certainly change the way you think.[105]

How to Change the Way You Think

Paul gives us the answer in 1 Thessalonians. In all circumstances, whatever we are facing, we need to choose joy. Joy over any other emotion that comes our way, and we should never stop praying. Be thankful for the small things and in the monumental blessings we receive, because *this is God's will for all Christians.*

Our joy, prayers, and thankfulness should not waver with the situations we face; but that being said, being joyful, praying continually, and giving thanks often goes against our biological tendencies. When we make a conscious choice to do what God says, we begin to see things from a new perspective: His perspective.

The Bible says that as the Spirit leads us, we will not *gratify*, which means to please or indulge, the desires of the flesh. (Galatians 5:16) In the book of Romans chapter 8, it talks a lot about this concerning our sinful nature/flesh, which is the fight between our body, mind, will, and emotions, compared to our spirit.

This is simply because those who are led by the Spirit are children of God (Romans 8:14), which is evident from the 'fruit' in our lives. The results of being controlled by the Holy Spirit and deciding to obey God's commands are found in Galatians 5:22. The 'Top Two' are:
1. Love
2. Joy

Joy is a choice, but it is a subsidiary, a by-product of something else: our experience of God's love, which in turn, produces love and joy in our lives.

> '*I love each of you with the same love that the Father loves me. You must continually let my love nourish your hearts. If you keep my commands, you will live in my love, just as I have kept my Father's commands, for I continually live nourished and empowered by his love. My purpose for telling you these things is so that the joy that I experience will fill your hearts with overflowing gladness*'! John 15:9-11 TPT

Regarding the second thing in receiving joy, some may be thinking that we lead busy lives and therefore to pray continuously on our knees to God seems unrealistic! Nevertheless, it is possible to have a prayerful approach by recognising our dependence on God, and that is why Paul says:

> '*Never stop praying*'. 1 Thessalonians 5:17

Prayer is merely reaching for God's hand and taking hold of it because we understand that no matter how deep the waters rise in life, He will never let us go.

> '*When you go through deep waters, I will be with you. When you go through rivers of difficulty, you will not drown…*'. Isaiah 43:2

That comes when we must realise that He is with us, no matter what our circumstances. And even when we can't feel Him, we are still determined to obey Him fully, because then our prayers become frequent, spontaneous, and direct. We start to include God in our lives throughout the day; not just for the times of need. And this is when we begin to pray without ceasing.

Finally, regarding choosing joy, Paul says to give thanks in all circumstances. I have never met joyful people who aren't thankful. Maybe they don't understand the season that they are currently in, but they are always thankful for the journey that God has them on, only because they get to experience it with God!

Giving thanks to God means that we might not comprehend everything in life, but we are thankful for the gifts that He has given us: for His everlasting love, His eternal goodness, and unmerited mercy:

> *'Whatever is good and perfect is a gift coming down to us from God our Father, who created all the lights in the heavens. He never changes or casts a shifting shadow'.* James 1:17

Without thankfulness, we become big-headed and selfish. We begin to believe that we have achieved everything on our own. Thankfulness keeps our hearts in a right relationship with the Provider of all good and perfect gifts.

Giving thanks also reminds us of God's goodness because we are all prone to longing and yearning for the things we don't have, but by giving thanks continually, we are prompted to see what we *do* have.

When we focus on blessings rather than wants, we are happier, and we become joyful because we realise that we could not even exist without God:

> 'Be thankful in all circumstances, for this is God's will for you who belong to Christ Jesus'. 1 Thessalonians 5:18

We are to be thankful not only for the things we like but for the circumstances we don't like. We can have thankful hearts toward God even when we do not feel thankful for the situation. We can grieve and still be thankful. We can hurt and always be thankful. We can be angry at sin and still be thankful toward God. That is what the Bible calls a *"sacrifice of praise"*:[106]

> 'Therefore, let us offer through Jesus a continual **sacrifice of praise** to God, proclaiming our allegiance to his name'. Hebrews 13:15

CHAPTER TWELVE

IT LOOKS GOOD ON YOU

Suit Up, My Friend

'When one takes on the Armour of God, fear retreats into the shadows'.
Brad Wilcox

Passionate about Metal

So far, we have looked at how joy can begin to bring a breakthrough in our lives, just because it allows us to focus on God. But for the final way to start to find freedom, I want to talk about something that I am most passionate about, because I feel that one of the reasons we can struggle with the concept of putting on the armour of God, each day, is because there are no physical pieces of metal to put on.

Therefore, it can feel almost meaningless to visualise us all suited up in the battledress of a soldier! It boils down to us having faith that our words have power and meaning in the natural sense, but also with the supernatural:

> *'Your words are so powerful that they will kill or give life...'.*
> Proverbs 18:21 TPT

Although this Scripture is with regards to the words we speak to others, what if we looked at it from the point of our own lives? That the words we voice to ourselves bring about life or death to our soul, and therefore praying over the armour of God brings the protection needed from the enemy's lies. Thus, when the enemy attacks our minds with his flaming arrows, they ricochet off our shield of faith like daises hitting a wall!

This is why I am so passionate about this piece of Scripture and why I believe that this is the key to winning the battles we face.

Put on the Armour of God: Now Fight

> *'All Scripture is inspired by God and is useful to teach us what is true and to make us realise what is wrong in our lives…'.*
> 2 Timothy 3:16

The armour of God is vital because even today some of us still have no clue about what the real fight in life is. I hear so often about issues that people are dealing with, but they reject the very notion that the enemy is the one at play.

There is no such thing as a random occurrence, but the enemy is so good at making things seem coincidental that once we realise his schemes, more often than not, some damage has already taken place.

There is no point playing ignorant to the things that are occurring around us just because we don't want to acknowledge the enemy. After all, can satan disable us should we unknowingly allow his influence to take hold of our lives, only because he masquerades as an angel of light (2 Corinthians 11:14)? He tries to deceive us by appearing to be attractive, good, and moral.

It is also important to understand that satan is not omnipresent. He can't be in different places at the same time—and therefore he uses the fallen angels, demons, to help him run this world.

This book was ultimately written to help free people from *Life's Greatest Battles*, which are the lies and deceit of satan. The outworking of them are the strongholds we have.

The god of this world, satan, (2 Corinthians 4:4) shows how powerful he can be as he was persuasive enough to convince a third of all angels to follow him in his rebellion. After all, they were all surrounded by God's presence and therefore knew who God was intimately:

> *'This great dragon—the ancient serpent called the devil, or satan, the one deceiving the whole world—was thrown down to the earth with all his angels'.* Revelation 12:9

Yet satan is still no match for the Holy Spirit; and the fact is, if one-third of the angels fell, that means there are still two-thirds of the angels left fighting for God in the spiritual realm.

Please let me clarify that this is not to say that satan rules the world entirely; God is still sovereign. But it does mean that God, in His infinite wisdom, has allowed satan to operate in this world within the limitations that God has set for him:

'...when Satan, the ruler of this world, will be cast out'.
John 12:31

The Bible states this verse, so we must remember that God has given the devil dominion over this world but for *unbelievers only.*

Believers are no longer under the rule of satan:

'For he has rescued us from the dominion of darkness and brought us into the kingdom of the Son he loves' Colossians 1:13 NIV

So why are there still so many Christians struggling with strongholds?

I believe it's because we will not acknowledge who satan is, so in turn, Scripture like the armour of God seems irrelevant.

'That sort of stuff just doesn't happen to me'.

Most of the battle is realising that we have an enemy. The rest is going to God in prayer, with our armour on, ready to fight in the natural, so in the supernatural, atmospheres are changed and the battles are won. That's when we experience the breakthrough in our lives.

Remember that we come from a place of victory, but the enemy wants us to think that we are defeated so he can try and leverage us. This is a lie.

We became victorious the day that Jesus entered our hearts. It just takes some of us longer to realise this and break free from the power that satan has over our lives, to walk in freedom.

On the other hand, some people overestimate satan's abilities, and they become fearful. Yet, satan is no match for God. Remember that death was defeated when Jesus chose to die for you and me. Therefore, Jesus holds the keys to life. God is simply waiting because He does not want anyone to be destroyed. (2 Peter 3:9)

And so, when we believe that we need to align our behaviour to what *all of the Word of God says*, the enemy then realises that we mean business.

When we choose to walk in victory as a son or daughter of the living God, whatever satan then tries to throw at us, the armour is there to protect and guard us so that we are strong enough to follow God into what He has called us for.

The enemy is real, but He is a spirit, just like God. He wants us to focus on the issues in our lives rather than the invisible forces that are generally causing them within the unseen world because then we forget to be on guard and it becomes about people and not about satan. We hate our spouse, our family, our colleagues, or even life:

> *'Be on guard. Stand firm in the faith. Be courageous. Be strong. And do everything with love'.* 1 Corinthians 16:13-14

As the Corinthian people waited on Paul's next visit, they were directed to be on guard against spiritual dangers; and they needed to stand firm in their faith, to be strong and courageous while doing everything with kindness and love. Today, as we wait for Christ, should we not follow the same instruction?

Life tells us that we can't get on with everyone. This again is a lie. We might not accept certain behaviours, but we are called to love everyone, as Christ loves us. (John 13:34)

The Last Fundamental Piece

In the last part of this chapter, I want to go into what the armour of God means, individually:[107]

> *'Therefore, put on every piece of God's armour so you will be able to resist the enemy in the time of evil. Then after the battle you will still be standing firm'*. Ephesians 6:13

Paul spoke this to the Church, but also to the whole body of Christ (the individuals within the Church) because we all need to be armed. Our strength is to fight together since all believers are now enemies of, and vulnerable to, satan's attacks, as inadvertently we are no longer on his side.

It is important to note that we need *every piece of armour* to be able to resist satan's attacks, to stand firm with God in the midst of it all. To withstand it all, it means we must depend on God's strength. This is not a fantasy. This is real. Good versus evil.

This is not another Hollywood movie, but the ultimate fight of our lives. God has provided His supernatural power by giving us the

Holy Spirit. His role is to guide us through life; but God also gave His armour to surround us.

The Belt of Truth and the Breastplate of Righteousness

> *'Stand your ground, putting on the belt of truth and the body armour of God's righteousness'.* Ephesians 6:14

God's truth is what brings light into our lives. That is why Paul says to put on the belt of truth first. The belt is underneath all of the armour because it was the primary thing that the Roman soldier put on. It holds up everything else. We need to always have this as central in our faith: that God is truth, because of who He is:

> *'All the paths of the Lord are mercy and truth…'.* Psalm 25:10 NKJV

As satan fights with deception and lies, we must have a daily commitment to being honest in all things. Falling in love with God's Word and reading it daily helps us realise what God honestly says because the belt is our core support within the armour. Sometimes this means that we will have to go against the grain by standing up for what is right in God's eyes. Being uncomfortable within our peer groups, friends, and even our families. This is all for our eternal rewards:

> *'If you go against the grain, you get splinters, regardless of which neighbourhood you're from, what your parents taught you, what schools you attended. But if you embrace the way God does things, there are wonderful payoffs'.* Romans 2:9 MSG

Interestingly, within the same sentence, Paul tells us about the breastplate of righteousness. These two parts of the armour go together, but righteousness is not something that any of us can reach. Perfection is not for humanity, only for God's glory:

'For everyone has sinned; we all fall short of God's glorious standard'. Romans 3:23

Righteousness is more about us living right and aligning with God's expectations. God does not expect us to be righteous because we just cannot do it, and this Scripture in Romans 3:23 confirms it.

Our self-worth and emotions are what satan attacks in that we are not good enough in God's eyes because then we will start to strive for God's approval continually, or looking around to see what others are doing, instead of trusting in what God is ultimately saying to us.

The Roman soldier's breastplate was so heavy that the weight of it would have exhausted them. How similar is that to us in the pursuit of perfection?

This world weighs us down that we don't have it, then tears us apart because we can't obtain it.

Yet, the armour shows us that God's belt, His truth, holds up His breastplate of righteousness so that we no longer need to have that pressure.

God expects us to be blameless in His eyes and that is a big difference.

This is where the Holy Spirit comes in because He enables us to do things that we could not do in our power. Whereby then we are moulded, shaped, or cleaned up by the Holy Spirit into the image of Christ.

God's righteousness is the armour's breastplate because it covers and protects our hearts to ensure we realise that God approves of us, as He loves us and sent His Son to die for us:

> *'A number of you know from experience what I'm talking about, for not so long ago you were on that list. Since then, you've been cleaned up and given a fresh start by Jesus, our Master, our Messiah, and by our God present in us, the Spirit'.* 1 Corinthians 6:11 MSG

> *'For it is God who works in you to will and to act in order to fulfill his good purpose. Do everything without grumbling or arguing, so that you may become blameless and pure, "children of God without fault in a warped and crooked generation." Then you will shine among them like stars in the sky as you hold firmly to the word of life'.* Philippians 2:13-16 NIV

The Shoes of Peace

> *'For shoes, put on the peace that comes from the Good News so that you will be fully prepared'.* Ephesians 6:15

You only need to watch the news each night to feel a sense of hopelessness. We can feel the pressure or the weight of what God asks us to do within our lifetime, and satan is always very good at telling us what we can't do or won't be able to achieve.

As I spoke about earlier, the enemy wants to take away our joy and to stop us in our tracks by listening to all of the negative responses that others give. He wants us to think we are crazy to believe that we can change the world, or a nation, a street, or a home, because he wants us to believe that telling others the Good News is worthless.

Remember from the first chapter, that if all the Christians rose up and shared the gospel, the great commission would be fulfilled within seven days! That is exciting to me because it gives me hope that is firm and secure in what God is asking us all to do:

> *'This hope is a strong and trustworthy anchor for our souls. It leads us through the curtain into God's inner sanctuary'.*
> Hebrews 6:19

The shoes of peace have a significant role as they anchor us to God. The Roman soldier had something called 'iron hobnails' hammered into the soles of their caligae (military sandal boots) to bring reinforcement or give traction when on difficult terrain. That meant the shoes were also an effective weapon against an enemy. Yet Paul shows us that peace and joy in any circumstance is an amazing weapon against satan, because no matter what life throws at us, or how many difficulties come our way, we are confident in whom we serve:

> *'I pray that God, the source of hope, will fill you completely with joy and peace because you trust in him. Then you will*

overflow with confident hope through the power of the Holy Spirit'. Romans 15:13

We live in a world that was overthrown by demonic forces that has led to so much sin against God and each other. The enemy hopes that we will be pushovers because of this fact!

This is where we need to realise that we cannot survive the storms in life without God's peace, because where there is uncertainty, there is no victory.

Doubt robs us of peace because our mind merely is then not focused on God:

> *'You will keep in perfect peace all who trust in you, all whose thoughts are fixed on you'!* Isaiah 26:3

Our shoes that God provides us with give us the stability to stand firm and allows us to keep our footing when everything around us might be like a tornado, bringing destruction in the midst of it all. Yet God's peace allows our minds to remain focused on Him so that we are guarded within the eye of the storm. The shoes will enable us to take one step at a time, to be able to move forward because the Gospel reminds us that this is not our real home, we are merely moving through until called home by God:

> *'So we don't look at the troubles we can see now; rather, we fix our gaze on things that cannot be seen. For the things we see now will soon be gone, but the things we cannot see will last forever'*. 2 Corinthians 4:18

> *'My home is in Heaven. I'm just travelling through this world'.*
> **Billy Graham**

When you are stressed, fearful, or have doubts, who or what do you run to? Friends, family, TV shows, an addiction, a pet? Or do you run to God? Your answer will show you the very reason why you may, or may not, have peace in your life right now.

The Shield of Faith

> *'In addition to all of these, hold up the shield of faith to stop the fiery arrows of the devil'.* Ephesians 6:16

Faith always needs to be current and continue operating in our lives.

Faith is seeing God's perspective beyond our natural circumstances. Faith believes, before we know the outcome, that victory will ultimately be ours; even when we still feel the pain and discomfort of events in our lives. Faith is putting into action what we speak in words, only because we believe that God's Word is the truth.

Faith speaks volumes regarding what we honestly think about God. If we step out in faith, then we are believing that God is going to move in our lives to bring that miracle, bring that healing, bring provision, bring whatever it is that we need; we walk into our destiny with the shoes of peace because of who we serve, God willing.

A seed of doubt about the faithfulness of God is what satan seeks to sow into our lives. Attacking us with insults through others about our faith, temptations will just so happen to cross our path, or we will find many setbacks come our way regarding the plans we have made.

The enemy fires discouragement and insecurity at us because satan wants the flaming arrows to be a distraction. The 'I'm not good enough' or 'God, are You really there?' arrows. How easy is it to forget, in the midst of everything that goes on, to remember that anything that goes against the very Word of God in our lives is the enemy trying to stop us from fulfilling what God is asking.

Flaming arrows were used to bring distraction against the soldiers, and if they could destroy anyone in the process, then all the better. The same with satan, he throws flaming arrows to distract us from God. If we are consumed with fear or insecurity, then we put all our attention on our emotions. This means that we are not advancing in the spiritual war that we are in, which is what satan wants. He wants to prevent us from fulfilling our God-given purpose because distraction means he has stopped us from walking in freedom.

This very book was about me stepping out in faith. There might be a more famous Christian author who could have written *Life's Greatest Battles*, yet God asked me to do it. Don't get me wrong; there have been times when I have questioned whether God *really* did ask me to do this. But deep down, I know the answer.

The point of faith is using the shield so that the arrows satan tries to hit us with don't impact our lives. It doesn't stop them from coming, and it doesn't mean that I am fearless; but with a

God-sized shield, the focus is on my protection in Him and not what the arrows are doing:

> '...*If God is for us, who can ever be against us'?* Romans 8:31

I have learnt that faith is just doing what is asked of me and letting God take care of the rest. The shield of faith is surrendering completely to God because it's not about trying harder; it's about trusting Him more,[108] and the more you realise how much God does love you, the easier it is for us to surrender to Him by walking by faith.

The Helmet of Salvation

> *'Put on salvation as your helmet...'.* Ephesians 6:17

Salvation is simplistic and beautiful in what God foretold. It is the ultimate love story, which brings us immediately into a loving relationship with the Father.

And yet, until you take salvation and unpack it to reveal its true identity in what it means to be a son or daughter of God, then we are not experiencing our true inheritance as heirs of Christ:

> *'So Christ has truly set us free. Now make sure that you stay free, and don't get tied up again in slavery to the law'.* Galatians 5:1

The Bible tells us that we are to renew our mind and that is precisely what salvation was meant to do: implement an entirely new way of thinking. The helmet protects our mind. That is what the enemy is ultimately after. He is going for gold, and the first prize in life for satan is to make us doubt God, Jesus, or even our salvation itself.

Salvation gives us our identity: it's who we are in Christ. At one time I thought the greatest miracle I could receive was provision from the Lord or even physical miracles. But I now know that the real miracles come from our mindset being changed, because that is when strongholds are torn down, through the very words within our Bibles; because when you know the truth, it really does set you free! (John 8:32)

The Sword of the Spirit

> *'...and take the sword of the Spirit, which is the word of God.'*
> Ephesians 6:17

I love the Word of God; it is has brought me through many seasons in my Christian life, and I know it will also continue to do so! Yet, my sword was a glorified coffee holder for many years because it lay there, collecting dust, thus it indeed it was not used in warfare.

The sword of the Spirit is the only piece of armour that is described by Paul, and it is the only weapon of attack within the list.

There are times when we need to be in the defensive posture with the enemy, but Paul reminds us that we do sometimes need to fight and this is with God's Word.

To me, it shows just how powerful the Word of God is. There is no other greater spiritual weapon. It's not conceivable because Paul would have mentioned it.

Remember when Jesus was being tempted in the desert? The Word of God was always His overpowering response to satan. Jesus heard from satan over and over, and yet still kept quoting the Scriptures back at the enemy. We need to do that! As a thought comes into our mind, we need to take hold of the Word of God, believe it and speak it out. Nothing is impossible for us to achieve when we take authority over our thoughts and change the way we think:

> 'We destroy arguments and every lofty opinion raised against the knowledge of God, and take every thought captive to obey Christ'. 2 Corinthians 10:5 ESV

How often do we ask ourselves if our thoughts line up with God's Word?

The arena is in our mind. I hope that I have been able to talk about this comprehensively for you to realise this. We need to get the power back that God gave to us.

> 'For God has not given us a spirit of fear, but of power and of love, and of a sound mind'. 2 Timothy 1:7 NKJV

Pray in the Spirit

> 'Pray in the Spirit at all times and on every occasion. Stay alert...'. Ephesians 6:18

This is the part that we seem to miss as Christians; but prayer is Activation 101 in our faith. It's the foundation, the very start of something beautiful.

Unfortunately for me, prayer was a means to an end. It was the final thing on my daily to-do list that never actually got done. Yet now, it has become a need, a want, and even a desire of my heart to pray and to speak to God on a daily basis.

Take a step back for a second and realise that praying to God is communicating with the Creator of the universe. To speak to God about anything is the most privileged opportunity of our lifetime, and one that we can't take for granted.

We cannot neglect prayer, as it is the means by which we draw spiritual strength from Him. Without prayer, without reliance upon God, our efforts at spiritual warfare are empty and futile. The full armour of God consists of truth, righteousness, the gospel, faith, salvation, the Word of God, and prayer. These are the tools God has given us, through which we can be spiritually victorious, overcoming satan's attacks and temptations.[109]

When we pray, connection develops. This connection then deepens as we commune with God so that we change from hearing about Him to experiencing Him intimately. A shift happens in the natural so that we desire God more, and His heart for not only others, but within our own lives as well.

We desire, we hunger and thirst for His presence, but as we do, a war will come. A war, as we have read, that will try to take our focus off God and His purpose for our lives. Therefore, as we put on the full armour of God, *no weapon formed against you shall prosper!* (Isaiah 54:17). Which means, when we focus on God and become obedient to Him, we are led by the Spirit to receive God's truth of who He is and who we are in Him, and that is when we truly win *Life's Greatest Battles.*

NOTES

Chapter One – What Is My Purpose?
1. Hackett, C. and McClendon, David; Pew Research Center (5 April 2017): Christians remain world's largest religious group but they are declining in Europe, Pew Research. Accessed 23 July 2019 www.pewresearch.org/facttank/2017/04/05/christians-remain-worldslargest-religious-group-but-they-are-declining-in-europe/
2. Got Questions, Cheap Grace. Accessed 24 July 2019 https://www.bing.com/search?q=got+questions+cheap+grace&src=IE-SearchBox&FORM=IESR4A&pc=EUPP_
3. Open Doors USA, Christian Persecution. Accessed 14 July 2019 https://www.opendoorsusa.org/christian-persecution/
4. Adapted from Bruce McDonald. 2014: *Prayer*. New Zealand: Lift Ministries.
5. Hybels, Bill and Mittelberg, Mark. 1994: *Becoming a Contagious Christian*. Grand Rapids, MI: Zondervan Publishing House, pp. 122-130.

Chapter Two – Does God Actually Exist?
6. An apologist is someone who argues about his or her faith. For more information, look at: www.gotquestions.org/what-is-an-apologist.html

7. Conner, Kevin J. 1980: *The Foundations of Christian Doctrine.* Portland, OR: City Christian Publishing, pp. 43-44, 15-19.
8. Kumar, Steve and Sarfati, Jonathan. 2013: *Christianity for Skeptics.* Powder Springs, GA, USA: Creation Books Publishers, pp. 17-22.
9. Grange, Robert. 1986: *Origins and Destiny.* Waco, TX: Word Books, p. 8.
10. Geisler, Norman. 1985: *False Gods of Our Time.* Eugene, OR: Harvest House, p. 52.
11. Catchpool, David. (9 November 2007) Inside the mind of a Killer, Creation Ministries International. Accessed 24 July 2019 www.creation.com/inside-the-mind-ofa-killer
12. Kumar and Sarfati, *Christianity for Skeptics,* p. 38.
13. McMullen, Emerson Thomas. 1998. Problems with chemical origins of life theories. Georgia Southern University. https://sites.google.com/a/georgiasouthern.edu/etmcmull/problems-with-chemical-origins-of-life-theories
14. Fobbs, Ollie. 2016: *The Conception of Conspiracy.* LuLu.com, p. 83.
15. Strobel, Lee. 1998: *The Case for Christ.* Grand Rapids, MI: Zondervan, p. 114.
16. Grant, Michael. 1992: *Jesus, An Historian's Review of the Gospels.* New York: Macmillan, pp. 199-200.
17. Komoszewski, J. Ed and Sawyer, M. James and Wallace, Daniel B. 2006: *Reinventing Jesus* .Grand Rapids, MI: Kregel, pp. 50-51.
18. Conner, Kevin J. *The Foundations of Christian Doctrine,* p. 44.
19. Kumar and Sarfati, *Christianity for Skeptics,* p. 41.
20. Mitchell, Stan. 2017: Sir William Ramsay and Luke the Historian, *Forthright Magazine.* Accessed 24 July 2019 http://

forthright.net/2017/12/05/sir-william-ramsay-andluke-the-historian/

21. Ramsay, Sir William. 1953: *The Bearing of Recent Discoveries on the Trustworthiness of the New Testament*. Grand Rapids, MI: Baker Book House, p. 222.
22. Strobel, Lee. *The Case for Christ*, p. 350.
23. Conner, Kevin J. *The Foundations of Christian Doctrine*, p. 26.
24. BibleStudyTools.com, Jesus...in every book of the Bible. Accessed 24 July 2019 https://www.biblestudytools.com/blogs/philip-nation/in-every-book-of-the-bible.html
25. CBN.com, Biblical Prophecies Fulfilled by Jesus. Accessed 24 July 2019. http://www1.cbn.com/biblestudy/biblical-prophecies-fulfilled-by-jesus
26. Conner, Kevin J. *The Foundations of Christian Doctrine*, p. 30.
27. Adapted from John Piper's, The Purpose and Perseverance of Faith. *Desiring God*, October 1999. Accessed 24 July 2019 https://www.desiringgod.org/messages/the-purpose-and-perseverance-of-faith

Chapter Three – Suffering with a Loving God

28. Lewis, C.S. 1969: *The Best of C.S Lewis*. New York: Iversen Associates, p. 429.
29. Gumbel, Nicky. 1994: *Searching Issues*. Eastbourne, UK: Kingsway Communications, p. 12.
30. Lewis, C.S. 1940/1996: *The Problem with Pain*. New York: Harper Collins, p. 91.
31. Gumbel, Nicky. *Searching Issues*, p. 23.
32. Jones, James. 2007: *Why do People Suffer?* Oxford, England: Lion Hudson PLC, p. 47.
33. The Voice of the Martyrs. 2002: *Extreme Devotion: The Voice of the Martyrs*. Nashville, TN: Thomas Nelson, p. 329.
34. Kumar and Sarfati. *Christianity for Skeptics*, p. 65.
35. Stott, John. 1986: *The Cross of Christ*. IVP, pp. 336-337.

Chapter Four – It's Them, Not Me

36. Bevere, John. 2014: *The Bait of Satan*. Florida: Charisma House, p. 5.
37. Battle Creek Church, How to overcome being easily offended. Accessed http://www.battlecreekchurch.com/home/180011666/180011666/180098931/How%20To%20Overcome%20Being%20Easily%20Offended.pdf
38. Bullying statistics, Bullying and suicide. Accessed 24 July 2019 http://www.bullyingstatistics.org/content/bullying-and-suicide.html
39. Robbins, Dr Dale A. *What People Ask About The Church – How Believers Should Handle Disputes and Offences*. 1990-2015: Nashville, TN: Victorious Publications, CB-29.
40. Bevere, *The Bait of Satan,* p. 128.

Chapter Five – Broken but Healed

41. Dictionary meaning: Definition of 'Heartbreak' from the online Cambridge Dictionary, © Cambridge University Press. Accessed 25 June 2019. https://dictionary.cambridge.org/dictionary/english/heartbreak. Used by permission.
42. Kurisheva, Julia and Riswadkar, Nakul. 2017: *Overcome Anxiety from Inside Out*. CreateSpace Independent Publishing Platform, p. 60.
43. Macchia, Stephen A. 2015: *Broken and Whole*. Illinois: InterVarsity Press, p. 192-193.
44. Story, Laura. 2015: *When God Doesn't Fix It*. USA: Creative Trust, p. 264.
45. Points taken from Broken things in the Bible. Accessed 24 July 2019 https://bible.org/illustration/broken-things-bible
46. Parts of paragraph taken from: https://www.gotquestions.org/broken-spirit-contrite-heart.html Accessed 24 July 2019
47. Story, Laura. *When God Doesn't Fix It,* p. 262.

48. Ibid., p. 265.
49. Chapman, Gary. *Love Languages*. Accessed 24 July 2019. http://www.5lovelanguages.com
50. Henry Cloud, Dr Henry and Townsend, Dr John. *How People Grow*. 2001: Grand Rapids, MI: Zondervan, p. 119.
51. Ibid., p. 120.

Chapter Six – Do you see me?
52. Paragraph has been reworked from Lisa Bevere's *Without Revival*. 2016: Grand Rapids, MI: Revel, p. 18.
53. Fox, Christina. 2013: *The Gospel Coalition, Dare not compare*. Accessed 24 July 2019 https://www.thegospelcoalition.org/article/dare-not-compare/
54. Definition of 'Keeping up with the Jones' from the online Cambridge English Dictionary,© Cambridge University Press. Accessed 25 June 2019 https://dictionary.cambridge.org/dictionary/english/keep-up-with-the-joneses Used by permission.
55. Thorn, Jen. 2018: The Comparison Game, Christianity.com. Accessed 24 July 2019 https://www.christianity.com/christian-life/spiritual-growth/thecomparison-game.html
56. Bevere, Lisa. 2016: *Without Revival*. Grand Rapids, MI: Revell, p. 48.
57. Reworked the paragraph from Lisa Bevere's *Without Revival*, p. 48.
58. Bevere, *Without Revival*, pp. 48-49.
59. Bevere, *Without Revival*, p. 85.
60. Aspects taken from Cindi McMenamin, Crosswalk.com, 4 ways to stop comparing yourself to others. 2017. Accessed 24 July 2019 https://www.crosswalk.com/faith/women/4-ways-to-stop-comparingyourself-to-others.html

Notes

61. Frank Sinatra, *Pick Yourself Up*. Accessed 24 July 2019 https://www.azlyrics.com/lyrics/franksinatra/pickyourselfup.html
62. Bevere, *Without Revival*, p. 90.

Chapter Seven – The Atomic Bomb

63. Paragraph adapted from the following article along with the following three points: What does the Bible say about expectations? Accessed 24 July 2019 https://www.gotquestions.org/Bible-expectations.html
64. Bevere, *Without Revival*, p. 159.
65. Paragraph adapted from Lisa Bevere, *Without Revival*, p. 161.
66. Caine, Christine. *Unashamed*. 2016: Grand Rapids, MI: Zondervan, p. 31.
67. Dewitt, Dan. 19 February 2018: The Gospel Coalition, The Difference between guilt and shame. Accessed 24 July 2019 https://www.thegospelcoalition.org/article/difference-between-guiltshame
68. Caine, *Unashamed*, p. 37.
69. Ibid.
70. Ibid., p. 38.
71. Ibid., p. 45.
72. Ibid., p. 56.
73. Ibid., p. 60.
74. Ibid., p. 183.
75. Bevere, *Without Revival*, p. 169.

Chapter Eight – Jesus' Number One Topic

76. Cortines, John and Baumer, Gregory. 2016: *God and Money*. Massachusetts: Rose Publishing, 01961-3473, p. 13.

77. Taken from What does the Bible say about managing your finances? Accessed 24 July 2019 https://www.gotquestions.org/managing-finances.html
78. de Jong, Paul. *God, Money & Me*. 2017: Auckland 1023: Life Resource International, 1023, p. 21.
79. Ibid., p. 34.
80. Adapted from Michael Packer, www.patch.com, Jesus talked most about…money, July 2011, Accessed 24 July 2019 https://patch.com/georgia/smyrna/jesus-talked-the-most-about-money
81. Hybels, Bill. 2014: *Simplify*, London: Hodder & Stoughton Ltd, p. 60.
82. Adapted from Bill Hybels' *Simplify*, p. 64-65.
83. Hybels, *Simplify*, p. 62.
84. Adapted from Jenn Fortner, 5 support raising lessons from the widow's olive oil, 25 August 2015. Accessed 24 July 2019 https://jennfortner.com/2015/08/25/5-support-raising-lessons-from-the-widows-olive-oil/
85. Adapted from Chris Green, The 4 Mistakes of the Rich Young Ruler, Sermon Central, January 2001. Accessed 24 July 2019 https://www.sermoncentral.com/sermons/the-4-mistakes-of-the-richyoung-ruler-chris-green-sermon-on-commitment-to-christ-32622
86. Hybels, *Simplify*, p. 66.
87. de Jong, *God, Money & Me*, p. 133.
88. Ibid., p. 130.
89. Hybels, *Simplify*, p. 72.

Chapter Nine – Yes, we Should Love Sex
90. Chamie, Joseph. 5 April 2018: IPS News, Premarital Sex: Increasing Worldwide. Accessed 24 July 2019 http://www.ipsnews.net/2018/04/premarital-sex-increasing-worldwide/

91. Statista, American's moral stance towards sex between unmarried persons in 2016, June 2016. Accessed 24 July 2019 https://www.statista.com/statistics/225947/americans-moral-stancetowards-intercourse-between-unmarried-partners/
92. Pew Research Centre, Religious Landscape Study, 2016. Accessed 24 July 2019 http://www.pewforum.org/religious-landscape-study/
93. Adapted from Mo Isom, *Sex, Jesus and the Conversations the Church Forgot.* 2018: Grand Rapids, MI: Baker Books, p. 23.
94. Ibid.
95. Adapted from Craig Harper, *Lifehack, Goal setting – the why behind the What.* Accessed 24 July 2019 https://www.lifehack.org/articles/lifestyle/goal-setting-the-why-behind-the-what.html
96. Adapted from Kevin J. Conner, *The Foundations of Christian Doctrine,* p. 126.
97. Parts taken from Andy Stanley's podcast Your Move – The New Rules for Love, Sex, and Dating, 2015.
98. Isom, Mo. *Sex, Jesus and the Conversations the Church Forgot,* p. 30.
99. National sexual violence resource centre, Statistics about sexual violence, 2015. Accessed 24 July 2019 https://www.nsvrc.org/sites/default/files/publications_nsvrc_factsheet_media-packet_statistics-about-sexual-violence_0.pdf
100. Moore, Phil. Straight to the Heart, 29 March 2018. Accessed 24 July 2019 http://philmoorelondon.com/post/20092207255/jesus-on-sex
101. Paragraph adapted from Phil Moore, Straight to the Heart, 29 March 2018. Accessed 24 July 2019 http://philmoorelondon.com/post/20092207255/jesus-on-sex

Chapter Ten – Rise and Shine

102. Stanley, Andy. Your Move, Who Needs God, Part Two – God's of the No Testament, April 2017.
103. Moore, Beth. 2010: Breaking Free. Nashville, TN: Living-Way Press, p. 215.
104. Got Questions, Giving Thanks to God. Accessed 24 July 2019 https://www.gotquestions.org/giving-thanks-to-God.html

Chapter Eleven – It Looks Good on You

105. Adapted from The Armour of God Bible Study, Priscilla Shirer, Lifeway Women, 2016. Accessed 24 July 2019 https://www.lifeway.com/en/product-family/armor-of-god?s_kw-cid=AL!4443!10!76553542946813!76553581444096&g-clid=&ef_id=XTJSwAAAAIQVdwnQ:20190724134431:s
106. Warren, Rick. 2002: *The Purpose Driven Life*. Grand Rapids, MI: Zondervan, p. 81.
107. Got Questions, What is the full armour of God? Accessed 24 July 2019 https://www.gotquestions.org/full-armor-of-God.html

ACKNOWLEDGMENTS

Thank you to Dr Shane Bermingham, Prophet Len Buttner, Ps Luke Brough and Ps Luka Robertson for being full of insight and wisdom. You have all played pivotal parts in my journey and will never truly know the impact that you have had in my life and my walk with God.

Thank you to my mentors, who continue to challenge my thinking and encourage me to continue to go after my God-given dreams.

To Aliza, Leighton, and Taryn, thank you for the invaluable coffee dates throughout this process, along with the recommendations through the initial writing process.

Vee, I love you for all that you are! Thank you for spiritually breaking ground for me and being a true warrior of Christ. 'Ehara taku toa, he takitahi, he toa takitini.'

To my parents, thank you for your coffee-making skills and for helping out where possible so that I could write 'just that little bit longer'. We have certainly had our ups and downs in life, but I respect and love you both beyond words.

To Kieren, my most favourite human being of all! Thank you for being my best friend and the love of my life. I cannot put into words how I feel, to know that you have not only believed in me throughout this whole period, but spoke truth and wisdom along the way. You continue to inspire me to go after God, unapologetically, and you lead our beautiful family in a way few can comprehend.

And most importantly, to God, thank You for opening my eyes to the wonders of being an author. You have given me freedom, a passion, and faith, which cannot be contained.

ABOUT THE AUTHOR

Cornish-born Rebecca Brand has a heart for everyone to be set free from the strongholds that this world demands are "normal." She has a passion for changing the world with hope, and desires for all to have an intimate relationship with Jesus. Rebecca has blogged for years, has spoken nationally and internationally, and moves in the prophetic. She thrives on single-shot lattes, chocolate, and quality time with family and friends. Rebecca lives in Auckland, New Zealand, with her husband, Kieren, daughter, Sarai, and their rescue dog, Nala.

If you wish to contact the author, visit:

www.rebeccabrand.org

Or connect on social media:

@rebecca.brand

@RebeccaBrand.page

INSPIRED TO WRITE A BOOK?

Contact
Maurice Wylie Media
Inspirational Christian Publisher

Based in Northern Ireland and distributing around the world.

www.MauriceWylieMedia.com

www.ingramcontent.com/pod-product-compliance
Lightning Source LLC
Chambersburg PA
CBHW071956070526
44583CB00015B/1213